The Twin Cities Explored

A Guide to Restaurants, Shops, Theaters, Museums, and Other Features

Indoor Garden —

Cover: Stone
Arch Bridge

Touch and See Room
Bell Museum of Natural History

The Twin Cities Explored

A Guide to Restaurants, Shops, Theaters, Museums, and Other Features

by Jean and John Ervin

THE ADAMS PRESS • Minneapolis

Contents

The Twin Cities Perceived: Eclectically and Subjectively

Guidebooks are proverbially prey to twin evils, of the chimera of objectivity and a comprehensiveness which ends in a kind of damp no-man's land, telling you a little bit about everything and ending by telling you nothing. Therefore, we assert at the outset the wholly subjective character of this guide to the Twin Cities, which results both from our highly personal selection of places, events, and groups, and from our opinions of them, wherein the reader will encounter no beige blandness. What we hope to provide is concrete information on the things which make life quite livable in the Cities. At a time when the very existence of urban areas is in doubt, we affirm our belief that residing in or visiting these cities can be a civilized experience. We may not be able to assert with Johnsonian positiveness that "the man who is tired of the Twin Cities is tired of life," but we write in the same spirit, convinced that the stimulations of art galleries, theater groups, dance, music, good dining, interesting historical sites, and other attractions of urban life offer a viable alternative to Thoreauvian retreat, and we hope to point out the precise possibilities to readers.

Writing in *Harper's Magazine* in 1969, John Fischer commented upon the high ambitions which citizens of Minnesota have for their community. "As a consequence although they have only two per cent of the country's population, they have built the fourth largest university system, several excellent liberal arts colleges, a symphony orchestra respected throughout the world, the Tyrone Guthrie Theater, and three art galleries of some distinction.'' All very true, but, like most outsiders, Fischer was seeing only the tip of the iceberg. We seek here to describe and appraise — selecting from what is in the tip but also from what is in less visible parts of the iceberg — those things that in one or more ways interest us, and that we hope will also interest our readers.

There are now five resident dance companies of some distinction. New crafts galleries are springing up around the cities, and in them as well as in the other small and the better-known galleries one can at times find shows of the sort sponsored by the more glamorous museums here. The Twin Cities have long supported music to an unusual degree — not only its longevity but the continuously high level of work by the Minnesota Symphony attest to that. But the success of the giant should not obscure the many other manifestations of good music, for two resident opera companies, the only resident chamber orchestra in the United States, the Bach Society, a Renaissance orchestral and vocal chamber group, and other fine ensembles all testify to the range of talent and support for music. An almost bewildering variety of theater groups provides everything from old-fashioned summer-stockish fare to highly ambitious and polished productions. There are shops which appeal to truly good taste, and while this is not the Promised Land of dining, neither is it a wilderness, for there are a few very good restaurants and many good ones. There are some historical sites, there are architecturally intriguing buildings. And still other places of interest exist.

Though no generalization will comfortably cover all categories, one at least will, and it is that there is more happening here than one would have dreamed. It is in the spirit of informing Twin Citians and visitors of our findings that we have written this guidebook.

A final note: The prices we quote herein will in many

8

cases change over time. We have cited a great many, however, as part of our effort to give concrete information to the reader.

Restaurants

Our goal here is to offer an extensive selection of restaurants for a mixed bag of pocketbooks, moods, and tastes. No attempt has been made to draw up an exhaustive bibliography of Twin Cities dining. We have (deliberately) left yawning voids in our list. You will not find, for one, those establishments where hauteur serves as a substitute for haute cuisine, where a flaming dish is thought to make up for a tepid soup. We are unblushing apostates, for we believe that diners should talk to each other and should not have to listen to the words of actors, singers, and comedians. We have included a number of interesting, little-known, out-of-the-way places not *because* of their modest size and self-effacing appearance, but for their quality, for a dedication to their avowed purpose, which is serving food. Again, as with other categories, we have been concrete; a specific meal is described and some attempt has been made to convey the general ambience. The Twin Cities are not yet a gastronome's dream. There remains a timidity, perhaps on the part of the diner as well as the restaurateur, a reliance on the safe middle way; but variety there is. Prices have been listed to give a general idea of the pocketbite, but the reader had best be realistic, they will undoubtedly climb the inflationary ladder with everything else. We have not hesitated to criticize adversely any aspects of the restaurants covered which are disappointing, but we have not included establishments which have virtually no redeeming feature. Finally, it must be noted that there are probably some good restaurants which we have not discovered, though this is not for want of trying.

Al's Breakfast

413 Fourteenth Avenue Southeast, Minneapolis. 331-9991.

The sign outside notes that this is the Dinkytown Branch of Al's Breakfast, but there is a gentle hyperbole at work here, for this is the one and only Al's. Nor could its flavor be easily reproduced elsewhere; it depends in part on the relaxed clientele of students and others who are willing (as they often must be) to wait in close quarters for a place at the long counter and who seem to feel a camaraderie. The menu shows a chef sitting comfortably in what looks like an alley — to us a pleasant mocking of the pretensions of so many restaurants in the Twin Cities. The interior of Al's Breakfast shows signs of being busy, but is perfectly clean. And there are even some handsome pieces of pottery among the things with which one is served. Service itself is efficient and amiable. The menu includes juices at 20¢ and 40¢, breakfast meats at 45¢ to 60¢, potatoes (30¢), toast (15¢), and English muffins with preserves (25¢). Eggs are variously offered: scrambled, they are 45¢ to 60¢, two-egg omelettes are 80¢ to $1.00, and both types include toast and coffee. The special Israeli breakfast consists of two scrambled eggs, kosher salami, onions, coffee, and toast — all for $1.20! Then there are many variations on the waffle theme: waffles with pecans are 80¢, waffle suzette (a waffle with sour cream and strawberries) is 95¢, and there are other possibilities. We had excellent waffles and syrup, and found the accompanying coffee as good as it should be in a breakfast restaurant. If you are particularly fortunate you may be treated to a lively panel discussion, with the staff and customers all participating.

Asuka Japanese Restaurant

24 South Seventh Street, Minneapolis. 336-3737.

Marked by colorful paper lanterns outside, and a few steps from the first-run movie area on Hennepin Avenue in downtown Minneapolis, is this very pleasant Japanese restaurant which opened in 1972. The proprietors have taken an ordinary retail shell and by adroit use of shoshi squares, handsome lamps, a mobile, and other elements have, while not obliterating the big room's less interesting past, made it suggestively Japanese. There is even a Japanese garden, created by artfully placing pebbles and backing them with a bamboo screen. And the whole effect is enhanced by the dulcet sounds of Japanese music.

Prices are reasonable and the menu is a varied one. There are nineteen dinner possibilities. Ten are called Asuka dinners, which are priced at $1.75 to $4.50 and are served with salad, steamed rice, soup, and a mild green Japanese tea. The main dishes for the Asuka dinners include a pleasantly light tempura (shrimp and vegetables fried in vegetable oil), a very satisfactory sukiyaki cooked at the table, steak or chicken teriyaki, and kushiyaki (beef, pork, and chicken interlaced with vegetables on a skewer and broiled). The remaining nine of the nineteen dinners are even more modestly priced, at $1.50 and $1.75. Among them are tendon and curried dishes. In sum, then, the menu is a good one, and the Japanese flair for understated décor is evident in the handiwork of the proprietors, who have made much of little in the design of what otherwise would probably be a featureless restaurant.

Becky's Cafeteria

1934 Hennepin Avenue, Minneapolis. 377-1600.

No pretence here. Becky's is honestly conservative, four-square "square." Interestingly, the meals we had at lunch one day were not at all bad, and we can recommend the cucumber-and-sour-cream salad, the home-baked goods, which include rolls and apple pie, and such beverages as an orange concoction made with an egg. And in the quite-adequate category are the braised sirloin and the tuna noodle casserole, as well as a strawberry shortcake which started out beautifully but became bogged down in a thick sauce. Other edibles available in the cafeteria line at lunch include juices at 20¢, salads from 18¢ to $1.15, beef loaf at 72¢, hash at 99¢, sirloin of beef pattie at 72¢, and other meat and fish dishes (none higher than $1.39), vegetables at 24¢ for the most part, desserts running up to 59¢. There are also sandwiches, which can be made to order. These modest prices and the cafeteria arrangement, which necessitates no tipping, make a meal here no burden to the pocketbook.

As for the atmosphere, it is, well, incredible. You enter to the deep, soft tones of an organ, and find that the Bible is open for you on a table near the entrance; the text for today is Jeremiah, XXXI. The serving room to the rear, where you take up position in the cafeteria queue, also contains Becky's Book Boutique, where suitable religious works are for sale, and a collection of very small pink furniture grouped about a small fountain. On the wall is a motto: "Love One Another." In the dining room there is a vast assortment of paintings, a glass-topped table with tea things under the glass, flags, a big gilt-edged mirror, and other reassuring decorations. The whole effect is one of being comfortable, and the families with children, the older people, and indeed some younger, longhaired ones whom we saw there testify to what must be its success. And to end on an upbeat — for, after all, it is worth trying Becky's straightforward cooking and its honesty — notice as well the excellent collection of antique copper tea kettles on display as you leave.

Bernie's

4212 West Lake Street, St. Louis Park. 927-8844.

This is a creditable delicatessen and restaurant. One enters through the shop, which sharpens the appetite, as do the bowls with dill pickles of good quality which grace the restaurant tables. Bernie's is rather featureless in appearance, but that is better than being hoked up, and the menu is extensive. We were there for lunch, and we found sandwiches from 85¢ to $3.50, eggs and omelettes at $1.25 to $2.30, a brace of cheese blintzes with sour cream for $1.40, delicatessen platters ranging in price from 95¢ to $2.95 (for example, corned beef, pastrami, soft salami, Swiss cheese, and potato salad can be brought together for $2.95), and a variety of desserts. Chinese dishes have also been laid on by the Woo-Boys (chow mein; chicken, egg, pork, or shrimp foo yong; and other entrées) for $1.65 to $3.75.

One of us had a luncheon special at $1.75, consisting of an excellent vegetable soup which was well stocked with meat and vegetables, a Hungarian stuffed cabbage which seemed to have a soupçon too much of paprika, and some robust rolls. There are other specials for $1.65 to $2.75. The other had a pastrami sandwich (these are $1.20 or $1.80, depending on size), and this was exemplary for the generosity with which it was filled with meat and for the warmth of the whole, though it was a trifle overspiced.

Black Forest Inn

1 East Twenty-sixth Street, Minneapolis. 823-2747.

Never mind the degree to which the Black Forest approx-imates a Central European inn, for its rough-hewn bar, with grey stoneware mugs, unpretentious dark-panelled dining room, German-Austro-Hungarian cooking by a German chef, and relaxed clientele and service — all exude gemütlichkeit. In the dining room, decorative heraldic shields are not taken too seriously by the management for they share wall space with an enormous photograph of formidable be-bosomed, be-bottomed, and be-ribboned dowagers — a Kaiserin and her entourage? But what makes the Black Forest Inn especially charming is the unselfconsciously tieless, sweatered, and shirtsleeved clientele, enjoying the food and beer, and engaged in lively talk. The German and other European specialties run from $2.35 to $5.25 and include shishkebob, rahm schnitzel, beef and veal goulashes, sauerbraten, wiener schnitzel, beef stroganoff, paprika schnitzel, and saure nieren. American meals — steak, chicken, fish, and seafood — run from $2.75 to 5.75. With each meal goes soup, vegetables, salad, bread, butter, and potatoes or noodles. One of us chose rouladen as an entrée, this being two rolls of beef stuffed with bacon, onion, carrot, pickle — a robust combination with a good, not too spicy sauce. The other order, of Hungarian goulash, had more dash and was served with sweet and sour red cabbage and noodles. The lentil soup was a tasty, thick workingman's concoction. A salad with herb, oil, and vinegar dressing was more delicate fare than the rest of the meal, but excellent too. A wide selection of beers (no other alcohol available) ought to include your favorite. We found the more than ample mugs of Lowenbrau on tap the best possible companion to this large, flavorful meal. A long sandwich menu, with prices from 65¢ to $3.25,

14

includes bratwurst, sauerbraten, some glamor girls such as crabmeat, grilled ham and Swiss cheese with mushroom sauce, and some plain Janes such as American cheese and hamburg.

Brave New Workshop
2605 Hennepin Avenue, Minneapolis. 377-2120.

Brave New Workshop Also
1430 Washington Avenue South, Minneapolis. 333-9687.

Dudley Riggs' Brave New Workshop — unlike, say, many an ice cream and ground beef emporium, whose dullness is dependably the same in all its branches — has two locations, each with a distinct personality. The present Hennepin Avenue cabaret was opened by Riggs after his unconventional restaurant on *East* Hennepin closed; it is largely a coffeehouse serving food in conjunction with its shows, but one need not attend a performance in order to sample the dobos torte and other pastries, the wide range of espresso coffees, the bagels, teas, and sandwiches. Heartier meals are now being dished out at the Washington Ave. Workshop at one end of the Cedar Avenue ambience, near the West Bank campus of the University of Minnesota, a neighborhood ripe with promise but one whose possibilities are being fulfilled very slowly in the visual sense. The first room in sight is the restaurant, which looks for all the world like a daguerreotype view of a nineteenth-century Chicago bar. But the feeling is of the real nineteenth century, and not that of an ersatz re-creation. The menu is a simple but interesting one, running to hearty soups, sandwiches on thickly sliced bread, fruit, cider and tea (in addition to the more conventional coffee), and tortes reminiscent of Sacher's in Vienna. Prices are modest, the staff not at all condescending. The restaurant is open for lunch and represents an excellent solution for those at the University or for downtown types who are not trying to impress anyone in an expense-account fashion and who are willing to forego preprandial drinks. Or a theater-supper is possible, served either in the restaurant before a performance, or at a table in the cavernous auditorium. (See Theater section for a discussion of the Workshop as theater.)

Casa Coronado

23 North Sixth Street, Minneapolis. 339-2212.

The homey-tawdry aspects of the atmosphere, created by the palms, the tiredly "festive" garlands looping around, and the huge butterfly on the wall, are a bit much to digest. As for the food, tacos and enchiladas of various kinds, while not remarkable Mexicana, are at least a welcome change from the prevailing Norte-Americanese of local eateries. The guacamole salad at $1.25 is an excellent luncheon dish. Corn chips and a hot hot sauce are served first, but our advice is to skip the sauce if you want a taste bud or two to be operable for the rest of the meal. The Fiesta Plate is a Mexican combo of taco, tostada, chile con queso, enchilada, tamale, Spanish rice, and coffee or tea, $3.00.

Similar combinations run from $2.25 to $5.00, and "pepito" dinners for diners under twelve years are priced at $1.75. The Coronado's menu is worth sampling. It is adequate. A few American dinners are available at reasonable prices. Of the wide variety of alcoholic drinks, the Coronado offers Mexican specialties such as variations on tequila, pitchers of Sangria and Mexican beers. However, be warned that mixed drinks may be chancy, as one of us found in ordering a Tom Collins before our lunch. In the evening singing trios provide entertainment.

Cecil's Back Room Restaurant

651 Cleveland Avenue South, St. Paul. 698-9792.

In a small, clattery room at the back of Cecil's Delicatessen one can dine on potato latke (pancake) with apple sauce and sour cream; homemade cabbage borscht, a sweet and sour blend much to be recommended; or loxburgers — lox, cream cheese, lettuce, and tomato — as well as the more usual deli-fare of blintzes, corned beef, etc. The menu is restricted as it is a small restaurant, but it is long on quality. The Cecil salad at $1.85 is a generous chopped mélange of eggs, meat, turkey, & vegetables, while the questionably named farmer's chop suey is made up of sour cream and vegetables. Omelets include the "backroom omelet" — eggs, green pepper, celery, onions, and cold meats — and side dishes of herring, gefilte fish, and knishes are available. The prices on dishes such as latke run from $1.45 up to the Taste of Everything sandwich at $2.35. Parking near Cecil's is easy and the service excellent.

Cedars of Lebanon

730 Highway 10, Blaine. 784-9967.

David George's Lebanese restaurant is proof of the old Chinese adage that "in good Chinese [Lebanese] restaurant you will find boss in kitchen cooking." For a number of years the Cedars has been serving consistently high-quality Middle Eastern foods in a tiny restaurant whose looks can best be described as American-Roadhouse-Lebanese-Jumble, where Hamm's beer signs compete with some truly interesting Lebanese jugs, shields, swords, etc. The atmosphere is enhanced by recorded Middle Eastern music, and extremely helpful waitresses will explain to you the mysteries of malfoof-mishay (stuffed cabbage leaves) and its cousin stuffed grape leaves, kibbee bil nyah (chopped raw sirloin with herbs), hoomoos bit tahini (chick peas mashed in garlic and oil), luban (a distant relative of commercial yogurt and much more interesting to know), cusa (stuffed zucchini), lubeeyah belaham (string beans in an interesting sauce), and shish kebab. The dinners are preceded by a wonderfully imaginative relish tray, with a summer salad the best of the many goodies.

Both Lebanese flat bread and hot bread are worth throwing away another week's calories on. And if you want to toss caution completely to the winds, end your meal with baklava and Turkish coffee. American meals of standard items are available. Prices for dinner are $4.00 to $5.50, and you can order à la carte. Reservations are strongly advised, especially on weekends.

Chateau de Paris

Hotel Dyckman, 27 South Sixth Street, Minneapolis. 332-7244.

The Chateau is a restaurant that merits praise for having for many years aimed at a French alternative to the standard Olde English look and vaguely Americo-Continental menu that many restaurateurs have depended upon to draw unadventurous clients. The atmosphere at the Chateau is relaxing and (sort of) Gallic. Of the three rooms the Wine Cellar is the most interesting with its high, dark-beamed ceiling, with bottles stacked along the walls, and with kegs, red cloths, and candles. The wine-bottle chandeliers are somewhat contrived. But a falling-off there has been in the cuisine over the years, although it is still worth a try as a variation on the local sameness. The luncheon bill of fare offers American dishes and Swedish meat balls in addition to some French possibilities. The coquille gratinee (scallops and mushrooms in a wine sauce) at $2.30 — which was in its better days one of the Chateau's old reliables, is now a gluey concoction indistinguishable from any other tasteless casserole in town. But the spaghetti Milanaise, in which ham, salami, beef tongue, and mushrooms are combined with the pasta (all for $2.10), has not wavered in its quality over the years. Other luncheon fare includes salads from $2.10 to $2.85 and there are still other dishes for $2.30 to $2.80. Carafes of table wine cost $1.25 to $2.00. For dinner, the Chateau offers mostly French specialties on its à la carte menu at prices in the $6.00 to $8.25 range, and there is a several-course group of dishes with wine at $5.75 all told: your choice of duck à l'orange, sole bonne femme, or coq au chablis, with salad, dessert, coffee, cigars, and mints. The range of possibilities in the restaurant's wine cellars is one of the most extensive in town. Service by the staff, some of whom have long experience at the Chateau, is competent.

Fireside Rice Bowl

1160 Northeast Fireside Drive, Fridley. 784-4402.

The ambience is unlikely, to say the least, but this is America, where our civilization is a mixed salad of borrowings. The name of the restaurant is accurate — a fireside to suggest an American institution, in this case a roadhouse of the proportions of a small auditorium, and a rice bowl to suggest Canton and Peking, whose traditions grace the menu. Do not be put off by the mundane appearance, for this is easily one of the four or five best restaurants in the Twin Cities area. In reserving a table by telephone, you can order for your party set meals at $4.00, $5.00, or $6.00, with dishes that include chicken marinated and then cooked in heavy paper to retain the juices, sweet and sour pork, delicately fried shrimp, superb egg rolls, a mélange of beef, water chestnuts, and pea pods, and another happy mix of chicken or lobster. None of these bears any resemblance to the American-Chinoiserie to which we are accustomed. An alternative to ordering the set meals (which are really worth taking a chance on for your first visit to the Fireside) is for two people to choose pressed duck, egg rolls, etc., from the menu. Both Cantonese and Peking duck are on hand. There are no spirituous liquors for sale. The Fireside Rice Bowl is best approached on Central Avenue and is north of its intersection with Highway 694. But it is actually on a side road running at right angles to the east of Central, and one is well advised to watch carefully for the not particularly conspicuous signs.

Fuji International

408 Cedar Avenue, Minneapolis. 333-7377.

At long last the West Bank has a beautifully appointed, inexpensive restaurant serving very creditable Japanese and other Asian foods. In July of 1972 the owner of the Fuji Ya opened this cafeteria-style restaurant not as a mirror of its more elegant downtown predecessor, but as one which fits the needs and pocketbooks of the University of Minnesota students and staff. The subtlety of the best of Japanese décor is here. A wall of shoshi paper runs along the street side, and its use above the cafeteria counter helps to soften and disperse the light. The most mundane cafeteria item, the listing of food, is artfully wrought on boards against a stone wall, which in turn echoes the dark tables and grey floor. Much use is made of plain woods, a false ceiling creating the effect of sitting in a Japanese garden. Oriental music and beautiful Japanese woodcuts aid in the illusion that one is dining in Tokyo. Tables in the front room are Western in style but not jammed in, while the back room has Japanese-style tables. Since we ate at the Fuji International on its second or third day of existence, its menu was necessarily restricted. The bulugogi sandwich of Korean beef at 95¢ had a distinctive taste, not as bland as our unadorned Western steers nor so hopped up as our beef in barbecue sauce. The chicken teriyaki (at $1.10 for a quarter chicken and $1.50 for a half) was very good, tender and marinated with the right amount of sauce. Served with both of these were onion rings delicately fried in batter, light and ungreasy. The suimoro seafood broth was bland, but since that seems to be characteristic of many Oriental soups perhaps our Western palates have been too long accustomed to broader culinary strokes and do not allow us to appreciate Eastern subtleties. Other listings: sukiyaki at $1.50, tendon:tempura on rice at $1.25, kushiyaki (skewered meats broiled with sauce) at $1.50. Several other broths and some teas are also available.

Fuji-Ya Restaurant

420 South First Street, Minneapolis. 336-8781.

Food is not only food, it is much else: people, the configuration of light and shade, memory. And of course it is ambience. The menu at the Fuji-ya tells us that the restaurant's name means "second to none" in Japanese, so perhaps the best way to describe the ambience in which one lunches or dines at the Fuji-ya is to say that in the Twin Cities it is, well, fuji-ya. The building overlooks the Mississippi River, though not its most pleasing bankside, for industry came early to this area and his scarcely been dislodged by time. But the water is there, and, more important, the interior of the Fuji-ya is satisfaction enough. The first dining room one encounters has high ceilings from which giant paper-covered lamps depend. Here there are tables and seats in the Western manner, with a serene, restrained, and altogether beautiful décor in wood, with translucent screens, and with red accents in the seat cushions to offset and actually heighten the basic restraint of the room. The next room, low-ceilinged and with windows which give on the river, is even more in the Japanese fashion: the tables are low and one sits crosslegged before them.

Waitresses in kimonos serve you, and prepare some of the dishes on hot plates on the table. One can preface or accompany the meal with sake, warm or on the rocks, with Japanese plum wine, or with Asahi lager beer. (Whiskey and other Western potables are discernible at the bar at the end of the first room.) The evening menu offers sukiyaki for those who like it, a light tempura shrimp, and other main dishes, each accompanied by pleasant skewered appetizers, a too-subtle broth in handsome lacquered bowls, a salad with tiny shrimp and a mild dressing, rice, and green tea, all for a not-unreasonable $4.50 to $7.50. There are also dishes prepared with teriyaki, a sauce made with soya, wine, and herbs — chicken teriyaki at $4.50 and steak teriyaki at $6.00. Rainbow trout shioyaki is $4.50. And there are many à la carte possibilities, including octopus in vinegar sauce ($2.00). The hot towels proferred before the meal are another very civilized touch.

Geno's Restaurant

670 Payne Avenue, St. Paul. 776-9274 or 776-9272.

Geno's is a modest-sized Italian restaurant with a varied but not huge menu, and at least the chef knows Italian cooking. For once a chicken cacciatore was cooked in dry Marsala wine, not drowned in tomato sauce, and the salad dressing was excellent. However, the spaghetti served with the chicken had a very so-so sauce. A Florentine antipasto was a meal in itself, an array of about four cheeses, pepperoni, hard salami, peppers, tomatoes, etc. The bread, advertised as homemade, was disappointingly close to American sawdust. However, the Chianti (a wine which can be extremely variable) was superb: a Melini at $2.50 a half bottle. Prices are moderate: spaghetti with various sauces runs from $1.85 to 2.50, ravioli $1.95 to 2.65, mostaccioli $1.85–2.50, pizzas $1.50 to 1.75, veal scallopini and chicken cacciatore $3.25. Geno's has a number of plain old American standbys: shrimp, walleyed pike, scallops, sirloin steak, and pork chops. Wine can be ordered by the glass or bottle, and a bar serves other drinks. The service is quiet and courteous. Go in shirtsleeves and feel comfortable.

Gopher Grill

Hotel St. Paul, 363 St. Peter Street, St. Paul. 222-4114.

If one were looking for a candidate for the Least Fitting Name of the Year, the recently re-opened Gopher Grill in the Hotel St. Paul would be among the leading contenders, for it is in actuality a quietly elegant, old-fashioned restaurant, belying the hick connotations of the appellation. While the menu is of the most conservative, play-it-safe variety, the GG has achieved that air of quiet good breeding so lacking in its flashier rivals which generally miss both elegance and good taste by overstatement. For one thing, its medium size is in its favor, and the ceiling is high so that the cacophony accompanying most restaurant meals is lacking. The decorator went easy on the opulence, indulging himself in heavy red drapes, and an elegant bar, but the net effect is that of a private club of bygone days. At lunchtime there were no flaming dishes in evidence (we count that as a very positive positive) and no music to talk over. The menus for lunch and dinner are small, but that may indicate that, instead of trying to be all things to all diners, the management hopes to do well a few dishes. Lunchtime entrées, ranging in price from $1.60 to $1.95, are served with soup or salad and coffee. The salmon steak was broiled without being dried out, and served with a subtle herb-butter sauce, although the Brussels sprouts must have spent the morning in the bath. The hot corned beef sandwich, served with tasty scalloped potatoes, was hearty, and the cucumber and onion salad a pleasant change from the usual offerings. Other items: pork hocks, with apple wine sauerkraut, a three-cheese omelet with Canadian bacon. While none of this will ever get more than a nod from a Michelin Guide, a pleasing air of home cooking prevails. Sandwiches and salads are standard and not expensive. Dinner offerings run from $3.75 to $4.50 for seafood and fish dishes; the misnamed Chef's Specialties include a large hamburger, chicken Kiev, beef stroganoff, and pork loin ribs. Prices are from $1.95 to $4.25. And the beef section is ample, running up to $6.95. As you can see, prices are below those of the local big-name places. The wine list is not huge but it offers a good sprinkling of domestic and imported reds, whites, and rosés. A B&G Beaujolais was served without a lot of fuss but with some know-how. Service was excellent. The maître d'hôtel is an old hand and the waiters are experienced and unharassed. All is low-keyed and pleasant. So if your taste runs to plain food, the Gopher Grill is one of the better buys in town.

Grand Café

South Main Street, Stillwater. 439-7263 for reservations.

One of the engaging things about the Twin Cities, its fringe, and beyond its fringe, is that at times one is surprised.

We had been visiting Stillwater for years, seeing it as essentially a sort of Yankee mill town, set on a handsome river (the St. Croix), and with some friendly looking, large-verandahed homes on the hills above Main Street. It is still all of these things, but it now also possesses in the Grand Café a large restaurant which is fairly convincingly Greek.

Its first floor is a dining room and, on weekends at least, has a buffet table. Upstairs, on the Saturday evening we were there, approximately the same dishes were served as we awaited the first performance of music and dance. (It is at times also possible to dine first downstairs and then repair upstairs for the entertainment; consult the management about details when you call for a reservation.) The one meal offered on Saturday evening upstairs began with hors d'oeuvres, including excellent feta (a goat cheese) and olives, a satisfactory chicken salad, and a conventional potato salad. This was followed by the pièce de résistance, a superb salad made with olive oil, feta, and olives. The main dish included moussaka (eggplant with a soufflé topping), and chopped beef apparently flavored with mint. These were interesting, but the lamb and chicken pieces which dominated the platter were less so. A small, rich piece of baklava was the dessert, and among the wines available were retsina (a resinated Greek wine) and demestica, a light red wine, rather thin in taste and unfortunately served cold. The demestica is $6.00 a bottle, and the standard meal is also $6.00 per person.

Of course, this price covers the entertainment. This had been promised, as the first Saturday performance, for 8 o'clock, but it did not get under way till after 8:30. The principal musician is Anestos Athanasiou, or Gyftof as he is known, and he is unquestionably a fine bouzouki player, with a repertoire which includes not only the expected songs from *Zorba the Greek* and *Never on Sunday* but also less

25

familiar compositions. He is accompanied by a drummer and a guitarist. Alas, the group is electrically amplified to the point in decibels where even the bouzouki, a subtle instrument, becomes clamorous. Next, with the trio accompanying her, appeared Scheherazade, an ample belly-dancer with remarkable hip muscles, who undulated her way among the tables, occasionally ruffling the thinning hair of middle-aged male customers. We understand that male or female clients sometimes are inspired, before or after Scheherazade's appearance, to leave their tables and dance, arms joined, in the Greek manner.

The décor upstairs is very plain and direct: It is a big room, high ceilinged, with draped windows, and with tables set in depth around a dance floor. Travel posters of Greece and a religious banner look down from the walls.

In sum, an interesting accomplishment, flawed a little, but well worth trying.

House of Wong

Roseville Center, 1163 Larpenteur Avenue West. 488-6687.

This is not really for the gourmet or Sinologist, but it is a good solution in many ways for a family dining out. Chinese décor is of course riper in color and design than Japanese, so one expects the strong reds and blacks that predominate at the House of Wong, but all the same the decorations seem a trifle more blunt and unrelieved by pleasant detail than is necessary. As for the menu, this is varied on both its American side and its Chinese side, as the following will attest: There are chow meins and chop suey, from $1.70 to $1.95, each served with steamed rice, oolong tea or coffee, and almond, sesame, or fortune cookies. Plus three types of eggs foo yong with the same side dishes, $1.80 to $2.35. Seven combination plates are available;

for $2.50 you can acquire chicken chow mein and chicken egg foo yong, with fried rice, dessert, and beverage, and there are other combination plates ranging in price from $2.50 to $3.35. But the most interesting portion of the Chinese menu is a group of Cantonese specialties, from which we chose Beef Chinatown, in which slices of beef are mixed with vegetables, and moo goo sai pan made with chicken. These are satisfactory, though a shade bland; with them were included rice, tea or coffee, and cookies, and the prices were under $3.00. There are, as well, appetizers priced from $1.25 to $4.40 — for example, Cantonese style barbeque roast pork at $1.60 and $3.30.

The menu and ambience, then, are adequate, but not what Henry Kissinger would write home about. As a resource for families, there is more to be said, however. Even though the restaurant seems popular, judging from the numbers on hand when we were there one Sunday noon, it is capable of handling a sizable clientele in its several rooms without the gruesome delays which some restaurants inflict, delays that always seem twice as long as is conceivable when young children are in the party. Further, the service by the staff was efficient. *And* the appetite of kids for hamburgers, french fries, soft drinks, and such is met by the management's thoughtful provision of same. Note: There is also take-out service.

International House of Foods Restaurant

6620 Lyndale Avenue South, Richfield. 861-7155.

The International House of Foods will vie with the best of an increasing number of Asian restaurants in the area. An abundance of North Chinese dishes offers a welcome variation on the predominantly Cantonese bent of Chinese cooking in this country, but in addition there are Australian,

Hawaiian, Formosan, Malaysian, Hong Kong, and Indian dishes. The range of prices on the made-to-order items is $2.50 to $7.50. First we had rumaki, a lovely hors d'oeuvre of chicken liver, water chestnut, and bacon, rolled and fried in batter. We found the sing song rice (whose name might more appropriately be hissing rice) a delicious mélange of tender chicken, pork, shrimp, vegetables, and those lovely black mushrooms; and Szechuan jar choy, a spicy North Chinese dish, a successful complement. The other offerings on the menu sounded just as tempting — for example, a North Chinese dish of pike baked in ginger sauce, Indian curries of chicken or shrimp which can be ordered hot, medium, or mild, pressed duck, lobster Cantonese, and Australian deep-dish abalone pie. Some of these items can be ordered on the Chinese Family Dinners for two or more. Each diner can order a different dish, and the greater the number in the party, the greater the selections. These cost $3.75 per person and include a few extras. The ubiquitous chow mein and chop suey are of course lurking around, as are some mundane American selections for the unadventurous. Appetizers include the aforementioned rumaki, egg rolls, and spice drops, running in price from $1.00 to $3.75. Soups are available, and North Chinese interpretations are reputed to be spicy. There are a few children's dinners for those under twelve, priced from $1.10 to $1.65. Service is excellent, and while the décor will never win any awards, it does not interfere with one's digestive tract either.

International Institute Luncheon

1694 Como Avenue, St. Paul. 647-0191.

The Institute's varied activities (for details, see miscellaneous section) include Wednesday luncheons served from 11:30 to 1:00 featuring a meal representative of a particular nation or a delightful mix of several, such as the International Luncheon at one point: "Venezuelan Chicken Pie, Italian Spinach, Saudi Arabia Munkaczinka, Nepal Banana Pudding." Other foods covered within a few months' span included Javanese, Irish, French, Spanish, Hawaiian, and Italian. We attended the French luncheon, and while the veal with mushrooms was really more an elegant stew than a delicate Parisian *veau*, it outdistanced any equivalent in a downtown restaurant where one might pay twice the price. The salad was actually served with a delicate dressing, and authentic French bread, strawberries, and coffee or tea topped off the meal. You should reserve your place before noon on Tuesday. The service is buffet style in an extremely pleasant, if church-suppery, atmosphere and is staffed by volunteer workers. There is no tipping. The price of the meal is $2.25.

Korai Kwan

466 North Lexington Parkway, St. Paul. 645-1694.

Adding a modest variation on the Asian cookery in the area, this small, unpretentious restaurant offers some distinctively Korean dishes as well as Cantonese, Japanese, and American-Chinoiserie. A typical Korean dinner might consist of barbecued chicken, kim-chi salad, soup, rice, and tea, all at $3.00. Others focus on meal-sized soups such as won ton, or tofu kuk (bean curd soup), with the kim-chi salad, rice, and tea at $2.25. Japanese dinners with pork cutlet or teriyaki are $3.00. Side orders of water chestnuts, black mushrooms, pea pods, and egg rolls are available. The barbecued chicken has a good pungent sauce which is somewhat heavier than Japanese versions. While mild, the tofu kuk possesses a distinct flavor, helped immensely by the black mushrooms. The most unusual feature was the kim-chi, a cooked, cold Chinese cabbage which had been doused for some time in a hot spicy marinade. The service was excellent and the look of the Korai is pleasant — a few lovely prints on the walls and a number of lush green plants were refreshingly low-keyed. A few grocery items such as seaweed and radish rolls are on hand, and orders can be taken out.

Lexington Restaurant and Cocktail Lounge

Grand and Lexington Avenues, St. Paul. 222-5878.

The Lexington is west of downtown St. Paul and in a largely residential region. Parking is not difficult, either in one of the two Lex. lots or streetside. After entering the too-small lobby, whose size is perhaps an encouragement to head for the bar if a table is not available, one encounters the principal dining room, which puts one in mind of the first-class dining saloon of a rather elegant steam packet plying American waters in the nineteenth century: red rugs, pink tablecloths, red velvet on walls and furniture, latticed windows, and low, chandeliered ceilings. As to the menu, for dinner there are many broiler dishes (steaks and lamb chops) ranging in price from $3.90 to $7.35; seafoods weighing in at $4.25 (scallops) to $9.75 (lobster tails); specialties, such as roast duck à l'orange at $5.25; and light possibilities, which make it within one's means to be accompanied by a hamburgiverous teenager (chopped sirloin is $1.75), and which also include salads and a few sandwiches. Many dishes have a salad (the Caesar, much gratinated, is all right) and potatoes as corollaries, and some lay on a vegetable (for example, peas with mushrooms) as well. About two specific dishes: the duck à l'orange is just acceptable and should be crispier and more flavorful, while the fresh broiled Columbia River salmon ($4.60) is robust with its sauce.

There is a medium-sized and -priced wine list, with some imported and some domestic possibilities, and we can recommend the full-bodied Côtes-du-Rhone among the reds. The bar is noisier than the dining room, appropriately; its paneling is attractive. And beyond it is still another pleasant dining room with a fire glowing on the grate the evening we were there. Reservations are probably advisable, though the only time a wait for a table proved necessary was for a Christmas office lunch, at which time the Lexington had evidently overbooked itself badly.

Lincoln Del

4100 West Lake Street, Minneapolis. 927-9738.

Lincoln Del West

5201 Wayzata Boulevard, Minneapolis. 544-3616.

As habitués of the old Lincoln Del we have found the newer Lincoln Del West equally fine in quality, the only difference being that the Lincoln Del West serves alcohol. Selecting anything as the Best Dish is impossible, for who can choose a king among monarchs? But here goes: Try starting with cold beet borscht, lox, or pickled herring and follow this with a hot pastrami or corned beef sandwich on onion roll (or any of the Del's other delicious breads). Or, instead, have the blintzes, which are not to be mentioned in the same breath with their frozen poor relations. For less delicatessen-minded members of your party the Del offers grilled chopped beef, spaghetti, and even weight-watchers' meals. The pickled beets which are served with sandwiches are just what they should be, as are the large quantities of coffee. All of this is a hard act to follow, but stop counting the calories and dive into one of the Del's pies, cakes, or pastries, any one of which might be from Sacher's or Demel's. Prices are moderate, although they seem inexpensive considering the quality of the food. The Del has a bakery section so that you can take home bagels, bobka, a variety of light and dark breads, and desserts. Service is friendly and efficient; the Del on West Lake is noisy-friendly, the younger sibling a bit more subdued.

Lowell Inn

102 North Second Street, Stillwater. 439-1100

General Washington never slept here, but he might well have wept here if he had been confronted with the self-styled Mt. Vernon of the West, for the over-decorated lobby and the even more elegant bordello-style cocktail lounge have little in common with eighteenth-century American decorative arts. However, the food in the American dining rooms represents the best of Americana, with such items as well-prepared broiled lobster tails, steak with morelles sauce, walleyed pike, and brook trout sautéed as it should be. The appetizers are truly appetizing, rolls are dependably warm, relishes delicious, and entrées, as indicated, know the length of their line. The Lowell management has escargots at $2.50, in addition to the more expectable fare. Prices for dinners range from $5.00 to $9.95. An alternative to the above menu is to be found in the Matterhorn Room, where diners are served a set meal centering on boeuf fondue and four kinds of wine. While the food is excellent, the wine is rather longer on quantity than on quality. The price is $12.50 per person for food and wine.

Mama Rosa's

1827 Riverside Avenue, Minneapolis. 335-7731.

An Italianate menu, the availability of light or dark beer

on tap or bottled, and its cheek-by-jowl accessibility for the West Bank campus of the University have together made Mama Rosa's one solution for lunch or dinner in this part of town. A pleasant surprise on entering is the changing exhibition of photographs or prints that hang in the lobby. The décor of the dining rooms is less successful; they are dark and rather improbably bowered by pendant leaves and grapes. From the menu, the Caesar salad and antipasto may be mentioned, and the paisano sandwich (lettuce, tomato, onion, cheese, coldcuts, and dressing) is ample and harmonious. Pizzas, pastas, steaks, and chicken are also available, as are other salads and sandwiches. The mugs of dark tap beer can be quaffed with some satisfaction because of the paucity of any beverage stronger than a nice cup of tea in most of the University precincts. A moderately stocked delicatessen/bakery adjoins the restaurant.

Mayslack's Bar and Grill

1428 Northeast Fourth Street, Minneapolis. 789-9862.

The luncheon atmosphere here is a compound of dim lighting (but that of a bar, not a tony restaurant), recorded polka music, signs proclaiming mottoes such as "Polish power," and, in general, directness and unpretentiousness. The premises consist of two rooms, one with tables, the other being the nerve center of the establishment where a bar, additional eating facilities, and the serving tables are. A queue extends frontdoorward from the serving tables if the place is busy, and the thing to do is get straightaway into line. The end result is acquisition, for a buck-eighty, of one of the house's specialties, beef or ham sandwiches of more than ample proportions. (They are also available at $1.95 to be taken out when there is no line.) Served with a sandwich, you can also pick up some of the garnishes and then head for a table or booth, where beer or other potables can be ordered. This is no place, then, for a quiet, genteel luncheon conversation, but it is — in the somewhat noisier, plainer American manner — reminiscent of that type of British public house which has a limited pub lunch.

McColl Pub

368 Jackson Street, St. Paul. 224-5421.

American banks are now very glassy and glossy in appearance, but there was a time when Strength and Continuity were the attributes that a bank wanted its architect to propose to the public. 368 Jackson Street is such a building, and, before descending to the McColl Pub in its cellar, linger for a moment across the street and study the façade with its columns, and also step inside the main building entrance to the right of McColl's doorway to see some admirable marble which has not been sacrificed to a redecorator's desires.

The Pub occupies the cellar, as noted, and what the cellar may once have looked like is not discernible. But the rooms of the Pub are themselves now cool-looking and handsomely unoverdecorated, so that the effect is that of interesting subterraneity. A good vestibule to a meal at McColl's is Heineken's beer, which is available on draft, and of course there are also other malt liquids, cocktails, highballs, etc. The wine list runs to sixteen varieties and includes a Bolla Bardolino and a Bolla Soave. There are in addition some French and domestic vintages and even a Portuguese wine.

The luncheon menu is extensive: The many sandwiches range in price from 75¢ to $2.35 and some of them are of the delicatessen persuasion. (The corned beef is well worth a try.) Omelettes and eggs run from 85¢ to $1.85. Or there are salads at $1.85 to $3.25, including for $2.25 a satisfactorily copious Land Bank salad in which masses of turkey, baked ham, salami, Swiss cheese slivers, tomato chunks, and a hardboiled egg surmount lettuce. You will find too collations of cold meats or cold fish, hot platters, steaks, and daily specials such as seafood newburg at $2.35 or Swedish meat balls at $1.95.

Monda's Restaurant

1047 Hudson Road, St. Paul. 774-0811.

The trouble with a place like Monda's is that it is so plain and so determinedly without pretense that in an assessment of Twin Cities restaurants it is apt to be overlooked. But it is doing its own thing well, offering up some Italian and American dishes in an exceptionally clean and well-run restaurant, and making no claim to anything else. One antipasto at $1.25 can easily be enough for two moderately hearty appetites before an order of lasagne, spaghetti, ravioli, or mostaciolli. The lasagne is one of the best local versions, although the sauce is a bit too peppery, but it is genuine, made-on-the-premises lasagne. The ravioli and mostaccioli are also the real thing and can be ordered half and half. Spaghettis can be had in various guises, with meatballs, chicken, mushrooms, etc. Prices on these meals run from $1.30 to $2.70. Monda's pizzas presumably appeal to pizza-enamored adolescents. Italian sandwiches such as the hot dago share a small portion of the menu with some American varieties, none priced at more than $1.00, and American expectables such as steak, fish, and chicken run from $1.50 to $4.95. Take-out orders of spaghetti and fried chicken seem reasonably priced. There is no alcohol. This is probably an excellent family dining place, as prices are low and there is no delay in the service, which is quietly courteous.

Normandy Inn

405 South Eighth Street, Minneapolis. 333-0223.

Like so many other local restaurants, the Normandy will never surprise you. It can best be described as a distillation of gastronomical Middle America, both in food and décor, offering an Old French variation on the English Inne style. But, from the number of meals we have eaten here over a decade, we can say that service is reliable, usually courteous, and the food generally acceptable. The Normandy specializes in steaks which vary in size and price, and they are cooked according to *your* specifications, not as a reflection of cook's sunny or black moods. The hearty Caesar salad is one of the more successful versions in town, here the popovers are warm and fresh, and the duckling, rock Cornish game hen, and chicken are variable in quality. As is already evident, you won't stumble onto any epicurean discoveries here, but at least the quality of the Normandy's cookery is fairly steady, if not infallible. Prices run from $4.25 up, $5.25+ for steaks, and meals include salad, entrée, potato, popovers, beverage. Wines and other alcoholic beverages available.

Nye's Polonaise Restaurant

112 East Hennepin Avenue, Minneapolis. 338-8921.

Do not run away when you drive up to Nye's and see, on the ugliest facade in the Upper Midwest, Chopin in bas relief batting out a few bars of a nocturne. Although the Polonaise Room is indistinguishable from the Chopin Room — both are noncommittal mid-twentieth-century salons, swathed in cavelike darkness — and most of the menu is indistinguishable from the pike, trout, steak all-around-town déjà vu, one can order genuine Polish

36

specialties of some merit at Nye's. Highly recommended are the pierogi (Polish ravioli) with sour cream, Polish sausage, sauerkraut, and golabki (stuffed cabbage rolls), all of which are served with hot bread. Luncheon entrées tend to be simplified versions of those served at dinner. Daily specialties are served at lunchtime — roast turkey, Swiss steak, finnan haddie, etc., and the ubiquitous short ribs. Entrées at lunch run around $1.70, although sandwiches and homemade chili are less expensive. For dinner, prices are higher, with a corresponding increase in the amount of food. For example, the Polonaise Plate features an hors d'oeuvres tray, pork hock, spare ribs, golabki, pierogi, potato dumpling, sauerkraut, dessert, and beverage — whew! — at $5.25. At dinner, prices for a few things do run as high as $6.75, but they tend to fall into the $3.50-to-$5.00 category. The result is well worth it, judging from our experiment with the Polish specialties and the pleasant, efficient service at lunch. (You should be warned, however, that there are "live" music and dancing at night.) Any sort of alcohol seems to be available, and Polish wines are on the menu.

Paula's Cocina

365 North Concord Street, South St. Paul. 455-9027.

In a drab building whose interior is best described as being in the American-booth style, you will find the finest Mexican food in the Twin Cities provided by the tender, loving care of Paula Garcia. The menu is varied but realistically manageable in size, with a special dinner featured each day the restaurant is open — such as steaks rancheros or sour cream enchiladas. On our visit, one of us ordered the Americano combination: a remarkably good cheese enchilada served first; then — sharing a plate harmoniously but not crowding each other into warring messiness — a tamale dressed in a corn husk as it should be and tasting for all the world like Toluca homecooking, beef and bean tacos in tortillas which seemed in their airy crispiness only barely related to fourth-generation American cousins, a creditable tostada, and rice; followed by coffee. This was $3.00. Our other order of chorizo tacos was equally good, hot for the Norte Americano palate but not unbearably so, and again the crisp tortilla shells were superb. With this we drank 3.2 beer, the only alcoholic beverage available, and supplying a nice contrast to the vigorous Mexican food. Other possibilities range from combination dinners such as a tostada or enchilada dinner with salad, coffee, and sherbet at $2.25; to an à la carte order of anything on the Americano combination; to huevos rancheros, with beans, tortillas, and coffee, at $1.80; to a guacamole dip (when available) or bean dip at $1.00; to Paula's homemade chile con carne at 75¢; etc. Desserts are on hand "when Paula is in the mood." That rates about four stars from us.

This is a small restaurant and if your arrival is untimely you must await your turn to be seated, so call in advance about the days it is open and about hours, and get there relatively early. Service is excellent, by the way, and there is air conditioning. In any event, *go — it is one of the best.*

Ricksha Café

5412 Penn Avenue South, Minneapolis. 922-3432.

For the dedicated epicure willing to anticipate the condition of his gastric juices at least twenty-four hours in advance, the management of the Ricksha Cafe will prepare a Formosan dinner (preferably for from six to twelve people). Since our one visit to the Ricksha was on a spur-of-the-moment basis we can only report that it seems worth planning ahead for the Formosan spread, the exact number of courses for which depends upon the number of persons in a party. Roasted shrimp, rice noodles, with seasonings somewhat different from mainland varieties, Bee Hoon — a mix of chicken, plum sauce and fresh ginger — form part of this promising meal. We can report from our own dinner there that the Ricksha is another small, carefully hovered-over restaurant in which you know that the owners are there and care about the quality of the food. The chicken almond ding, with mushrooms, pea pods, water chestnuts, and of course chicken and almonds, was a delightfully subtle blend of those elements. More self assertive, and a nice contrast for food-sharers, was the beef–green pepper–tomato mix, a Cantonese dish with spiced black bean sauce. These were part of a group of special Cantonese foods which ran from $2.45 to $2.55. Others were variations on the chicken and beef, and a shrimp dish in lobster sauce sounded good. Appetizers such as egg roll are from $1.25 to $1.55, soups 40¢ to 95¢. The inevitable chow meins and chop sueys range from $1.05 to $1.95, and American sandwiches and a few other meals are there. There is a lively take-out service. It is probably best to call ahead both for take-out service or for a table as it is small restaurant. Overlook the décor, which is an uninteresting Sino-American blend.

Rocco's

1179 East Minnehaha Avenue, at Duluth Avenue, St. Paul. 776-9157.

The most interesting of the restaurants of an Italian per-suasion in the Twin Cities, Rocco's is a pleasant place of moderate dimensions, with friendly service, and though the dishes took some time in arriving this must have been because of care in their preparation. The luncheon menu includes a good lasagne at $1.95, which we tried, ravioli and chicken cacciatore, each $1.95, and veal scallopini at

$2.10. Most of these are assisted by a nice salad, a beverage, and genuine Italian-style bread. Salads as separate items run from 35¢ to $1.85, and we can vouch for the antipasto, a heaping assortment of artichokes, meats, lettuce, and much else — the most convincing antipasto in the two cities. Also on the luncheon menu are American dishes, sandwiches, pizzas, added ravioli entries, spaghetti possibilities, etc. A slightly larger Italian menu and a big American selection are available in the evening.

Rusciano's

328 South Third Street, Minneapolis. 332-6872 or 332-3675.

A friendly place, with the management normally in shirtsleeves and the staff quite amiable. Italian dishes are a specialty, though it must be said that the tomato sauce for the pastas is too hopped up. American meals are available also, and the lounge with its bar could scarcely be more American. Traverse it, and if you are there in the evening you will usually find a quiet dining room with Italian-café-style tablecloths. At noon more customers are there and the result is inevitably a somewhat less relaxed atmosphere. Antipastos are excellent and more than ample in size. Minestrone and sandwiches can be recommended, pizzas exist, the rum cake with whipped cream is the ideal dessert. A carafe of table wine at $1.50 at noon or an excellent imported Valpolicella or Bardolino at night is notable, because most restaurants in the Twin Cities, when they have imported wine, have been seduced by the glamor of French labels and make only them available. Rusciano's prices are moderate. For a number of years now it has offered an Italian smorgasbord on Saturday nights at $3.75 and on Wednesdays a special dinner with all the spaghetti you can eat and all the wine you can drink at $3.25.

St. Paul Hilton Restaurants

11 East Kellogg Boulevard, St. Paul. 222-7711.

The Hilton is very much *there*, for it is one of the dominant edifices on the edge of downtown St. Paul near the Mississippi River. Although it has become fashionable to be a member of the "World Hilton-Hating" club, the view from the top of the St. Paul version of this ubiquitous chain is well worth at least one ascent to the twenty-second floor in the glass-fronted elevator. Arrived at the *Top of the Hilton*, whose décor can be described as "good corny," one may wish first to have a drink at the bar or at a table and study the river. (Aperitives like Dubonnet and Pernod are sensibly priced at $1.00, by the way.) Many of the dining tables also offer views of the city and the river valley. In daylight the prospect would not have inspired a Pirenesi veduta: many of the buildings one sees are warehouses and factories and even the small municipal airport and the houses (though possessing ambient green areas) are blunt and angular in appearance. However, in good weather a commercial barge, the local sternwheeler, or a rower in a racing shell bending to his oars or drifting as if an Eakins painting — these are pleasant riparian sights. In full darkness, the buildings except for their lights have disappeared and the St. Paul Cathedral is gaudily aglow. Best of all, arrive just before dusk and then the buildings in view begin to dissolve and the land and water contours are seen with a painter's sfumato effect. Gradually, soft lights go on, not to become bright and hard till full darkness falls.

At noon the dining room at the Top serves an international buffet. Besides the tables near the windows, there is at the center of the floor a slowly revolving carousel platform which could be an attraction for younger members of the family. Prices generally are moderate to lowish high, so that one need not mortgage anything to take a family to dine here. The dinner menu includes a main course, such as a chopped steak or a pleasant though not remarkable veal Cordon Bleu or Idaho trout almondine, with salad and potato, at $4.25, with other possibilities being priced up to $7.50. Shrimp, onion soup, escargots at $1.85 and other appetizers are extra, as are such desserts (at only 75¢) as baked Alaska or pastries from a cart. A specialty is the Carousel Gourmet Dinner at a total of $18.50 for two, which offers escargots, tossed salad, Chateaubriand, vegetables, a half bottle of vin Rosé, and pastry. The wine list has a fair number of domestic and imported choices. Candles on the table at dinner and a pianist, followed by a quartet playing popular music, complete the setting.

Returned to the lobby floor, you may have to fight your way through a Junior Chamber of Commerce crowd whose convention has been held in the Hilton. An alternative for dinner is *Don the Beachcomber's* Restaurant on the lobby level. This has a rather contrived Polynesian look replete with cocoanut and carved-post effects. Appetizers range in type and price from tapa-tapa (skewered marinated beef) at 75¢ to beachcomber barbecued chicken at $2.50; Cantonese pork, peas and chestnuts, Mandarin duck, chicken manuu and other dishes are available à la carte at $3.25 to $5.50. Special drinks are in the $1.10 to $2.50 range. We found the atmosphere heavy and a dinner there unremarkable.

Salvatore's

1 South Seventh Street, Minneapolis. 332-1852.

This small newcomer to the roster of Twin Cities restaurants sounded more promising than it actually was, for, on hearing that its owner is from Northern Italy, we looked for a change from the over-tomatoey local Italian cuisine.

We tried risi e bisi, rice with peas, cheese, bacon, green onion, and mushrooms, but a too-heavy stress on the bacon overpowers what can be, in Italy, a subtle mélange of flavors. The manicotti had what appeared to be a bread stuffing, which the cook only partially covered with mozarella. Alas, it had less flavor than the manicotti to which we had grown accustomed. The salad, however, was excellent — really subtle herbs, oil, and vinegar combined to make the greens and tomatoes taste as they should — and the garlic bread was tasty. The prices for these meals ran around $3.00. For $4.95 one can purchase a seven-course meal which consists of soup, salad, spaghetti, tomatoes with cheese, a veal or chicken entrée, a worthy selection of fresh fruit, pastry, and beverage. We did not try the desserts, such as cherries Portofino and Italian crème caramel, but at least they ring a refreshing change on the usual post-prandial *bland*ishments. We chose instead to end our meal with a lovely cappucino, very evocative of Italian caffès. Aesthetically, Salvatore's has avoided the worst of restaurant horror-décor, and its size is conducive to digesting food. But what the canned music was intended to do for our internal economy, 'tis hard to say. The service was excellent.

Sammy D's

1407 Fourth Street Southeast, Minneapolis. 331-9630.

An atmosphere of Italian bonhomie pervades this popular restaurant in the Dinkytown area of Minneapolis, near the University. Three sculptured putti are framed in arches in the façade of the establishment on Fourth Street, and colored lights play on another sculpture in the second (and quieter) of the two rooms. The first room is noisier, but pleasantly so, because it gives upon the kitchen behind a serving counter. One can also observe at least two notes of rather robust piety: among the decorations are a good likeness of Pope John XXIII and a banner proposing that "Faith perceives truth sooner than experience can"! The menu offers sandwiches in a price range from 40¢ to $1.45 (including a hotdog which our seven-year-old son pronounced good, and a sweet pepper sandwich which is flavorful but slightly greasy), various pastas at $1.10 to $1.85, a very satisfactory antipasto with much beef and sausage, and desserts. There is also a Fiesta Dinner — peaches in wine sauce, chicken cacciatore, and other dishes, making seven courses altogether — which must be ordered a week in advance and be served to at least four. Dinkytown denizens will have tried both Sammy D's and Vescio's, for each has its points. Perhaps most noticeable is that Vescio's has a more extensive menu. On the other hand, Sammy D's has a more engaging and less austere look inside and out. Both are very matey, which is just right for a shopping area cheek by jowl with a university. Starchiness would be unthinkable.

Seven Markets

45 South Seventh Street, Minneapolis. 333-2181.

If you are in search of la vraie cuisine française, or cucina Italiana, you won't find it at the Seven Markets, but for an adequate American imitation of them as well as Mexican or English dishes (though who, including the English ever pretended that their cooking was anything to be more than endured?) try this pleasantly decorated and well-run cafeteria. You can eat a less expensive and more palatable lunch here than at many of the pretenteries in the neighborhood. The French section features crêpes filled with beef hash or chicken and mushrooms (both very good), or you can get dessert crêpes, but the latter were filled with ersatz strawberry something or other, which ruined an otherwise delicate pancake. French onion soup is good at 35¢ a serving. While the salad dressings of oil and vinegar are actually on hand, the container for the salad was so small that it was nearly impossible to eat from it. More successful than the French offerings were the Mexican entries. The Mexican sample plate at $1.46 contained cheese and beef enchiladas, and a taco filled with tasty items. Have a glass of wine at a very reasonable 35¢.

Sheraton-Ritz Hotel Restaurants

315 Nicollet Mall, Minneapolis. 336-5711.

There are two restaurants in this, the most elegant of the city's hotels, and you may wish to preface a visit to either by a drink in the Golliwog Lounge at the top of the building. As for the restaurants, our preference is for the Cheshire Cheese on the second (or lobby) floor, where the management wisely decided not to copy the uncopyable original public house of that name in London, with its old wood, its sawdust-strewn floors, and its pleasant clamor. The Sheraton version consists of a single large dining room, with plenty of light from windows overlooking the hotel's terrace. While the dark wood of the Sheraton's Cheshire Cheese contrasts well with the vivid red of the cloths and carpeting, things have gotten out of hand in the case of the large glass picture panels between the windows and in the case of the "quaint" costumes worn by the staff. The service can be slow at lunch, even when one arrives before noon. A satisfactory glass of wine or a Watney ale (an English specialty of good amber color and firm flavor, available in a glass or as a half-yard or yard) passes the time till the food arrives. As for the food, one can choose from sandwiches ($1.65 to $2.45); a bill of fare including baked macaroni, or liver and bacon, halibut, an omelette, or ham and eggs, ranging in price from $1.85 to $3.50; a group of grilled dishes, such as chopped steak at $1.95 to $3.50; the "Stew Pot" specialty of the day at $2.40, which on one Friday was a nice seafood curry with steamed rice; and choices at $2.00 to $3.25 from the cold board, such as the hearty Dickinson's platter at $3.00, a concoction involving chunks of fresh tuna fish, black and green olives, and mushrooms, but with a spicy dressing which rather overstated itself. Good crusty breads, coffee, and, where appropriate, a green salad accompany many of these meals. Unhurried luncheoners may wish to sample the desserts (some of them from a pastry cart) which are prepared in the restaurant's pastry shop. In the evening dinners run in price from $4.65 to $8.75. It is very much on the safe and sunny side of the fence, with lamb chops, duckling, steak, lobster, chicken, and veal.

On the hotel's ground floor athwart the swimming pool and terrace, but indoors, is La Brasserie, which we have found a possibility, but a less interesting one than the Cheshire Cheese. The price range is similar to that of the Cheese, both being moderate to expensive, and the décor is satisfactory. The Brasserie's menu is not especially Gallic.

Sibley Tea House

Highway 13, Mendota. 452-1040.

Not to be confused with the historic Sibley House, but situated near it and pleasant in itself, is the Sibley Tea House. Pleasant enough, in fact, so that one might wish to lunch or dine there whether or not a visit to the Sibley House is also planned. Allot yourself two hours if you are in downtown St. Paul or Minneapolis, shake the city from your shoulders, and drive to Mendota. The Tea House is interestingly old (in Minnesota-time), and it is set near the highway but with a spacious lawn adjacent and visible through windows from some of its tables, so a visit on a good day is preferred. And best of all, the autumn foliage along the river provides the setting for a pre- and postprandial drive. Or, regardless of the weather, if you are going to Mendota for New Orleans music at the Emporium of Jazz (see the entry in our Music section), a dinner beforehand at the Tea House would be pleasant. Each night a different dinner is served — roast pork, pike, beef, and lamb alternating and sometimes sharing the menu. With this is served fruit juice or melon, salad, rolls and a beverage, all a very good buy at approximately $4.00. At lunch, prices run from $2.00 to $2.75 with fine chicken and shrimp salads and ham rolls topping the list of our favorites. It is tearoomy, serving sweet rolls with lunch, but don't let that deter you, for there is a concentration on good, plain food, without fanfare.

Taj Mahal

1034 Nicollet Avenue, Minneapolis. 332-9952.

While the Twin Cities have some distance to travel before they enter a gastronome's list of cities to be visited the growing number of Asian restaurants gives one hope. In July of '72 the Taj Mahal's spicy menu put some much-needed bite into downtown Minneapolis cuisine, with such dishes as Taj Tanduri (chicken with spices), chicken, beef, lamb or shrimp curries, keema alo (ground beef with potato), saag (beef or lamb with spinach in spices, much better than it sounds), mattan paneer (cheese and peas), channas (chick peas curried), and various yogurt combinations. In order to sample a fairly wide variety we tried a kaleidoscopic luncheon of side dishes and found all of them interesting, with channas too hot a curry for our Western palates, but undoubtedly true to its orgins. The saag was particularly tasty, less hot than the curry, but spicy, and the yogurt and potato excellent. Undoubtedly, the lamb curry had been somewhat lowered in pungency to accommodate Nicollet Ave tastes, and very good it was. Be certain to order one of the Indian breads. The one we chose consisted of two large round, freshly fried, absolutely delicious pieces. The breads run around 40¢ a serving, and pilafs are slightly more. At lunch time the prices of meals are $2.50 for a complete meal of Taj tanduri or a curry, but the side dishes run from 75¢ to $1.35. The dinner menu is slightly enlarged and the prices somewhat higher, but none exceeds $3.85. Some realistic concessions to totally American taste buds are made, with American sandwiches and meals of no particular interest being offered. There is also a vegetarian meal which sounds Indian in its bent. In its early weeks, the Taj management had not done much to eradicate its noncommittal coffee-shop look, but perhaps the owners in time will dream up ways to waft us a bit closer to Delhi.

Tokyo Restaurant

1325 Fourth Street Southeast, Minneapolis. 331-9997.

Dinkytown is not Tokyo's Ginza, but because a moderate number of the University crowd who noonwards flock to it want something more remarkable than a hamburger, this small restaurant with inexpensive Japanese food attracts many clients. In point of fact, the sixty or so customers who represent the restaurant's capacity must be sinuous and lithe to stay out of each other's sukiyaki, for the tables and counters are close together. Among the specialties are tendon (fried shrimp nesting in lettuce and rice), chicken teriyaki, and sukiyaki deluxe, and these range in their degree of success from poor (tendon) to good (sukiyaki). Tea and fortune cookies are staples. The place vibrates with talk and there seems to be no jukebox or muzak, which is one of its pleasant features.

Vescio's

406 Fourteenth Avenue Southeast, Minneapolis. 378-1747.

A durable Dinkytown institution which does a lively trade in Italianate lunches and dinners in three comfortable but unpretentious dining rooms. The menu includes pizzas, sandwiches, pasta dishes, and salads. Among the sandwiches are the capacious Big Boy at $1.50 and the single or double Toni (sausage or beef, sweet peppers, and lettuce, all on toast). Salads include a pleasant antipasto, a Caesar, and a sweet pepper salad, the latter at a modest 60¢. The dressings have been so successful that, in addition to their availability on the salads, they are bottled at the restaurant and sold to customers at the cashier's counter and are also purveyed at Red Owl stores. Business at Vescio's is brisk at normal luncheon hours and one may wish to arrive slightly before or after those hours or call to reserve a table — preferably in the third dining room, farthest from the entrance and thus the snuggest.

Shops

In an age of the supergeneralstore, when the supermarket/ department store/drugstore may be the most convenient resource for the busy shopper, everyone complains of the side effects of these mammoths: a facelessness, a lack of individuality, the disappearance of a defined personality. What follows represents a culling of the Twin Cities' shops, and in most cases those we have described manifest some of this lost individuality. They were chosen also for a particular interest, such as a focus on imported goods, or for an esthetically high quality of merchandise, or because they have a concentration of useful objects not usually found in one place. This is a personalized guide to shopping in out-of-the-way places, a verbal map to help you ferret out a piece of handmade pottery, some foreign foodstuffs, a wall hanging, a caftan, a well-designed silver bracelet, a merino sheepskin rug — and to do so mostly in pleasant places with a personality, rather than in (however convenient they are) bland superstores. Note that some of the museum shops and the galleries described in our Museum and Art Gallery section also have interesting objects of this type for sale, as well as works of art.

Carbone Brothers Grocery and Liquor Store

335 University Avenue East, St. Paul. 224-1816.

Jack Ervin likes any kind of food, just as long as it is Italiano in leaning, so any number of times a year Jean Ervin drives down University Avenue to Carbone's to purchase staples such as freshly grated cheese, pastas of every conceivable shape (shells, wheels, rotini, linguine, green noodles, lasagne noodles, manicotti, rosamarina), imported olive oil in almost any size of container, Medaglia d'Oro coffee, small, medium, large or Paul Bunyan cans of tomato paste, pepperoncini, and calamata olives. Carbone's is one of the few local spots where one can almost always rely on finding fresh ricotta cheese for lasagne or manicotti. Other not-to-be-ignored standbys are the fon-

50

tanelle, provolone, mozarella, and gorgonzola cheeses, hard
salamis, and Italian bread. Although we have never tried
them, you might want to venture into the frozen raviolis
and other frozen pastas. When you have exhausted the possibilities of the grocery side but before your wallet is
similarly done in, step across to the liquor department to
select the appropriate aperitivo, such as Punt e Mes, Cam-
pari, or bianco vermouth, and to drink with your food pick
up a Bardolino, a Soave, a Valpolicella. In place of dessert
try a glass of that sexy Sicilian indulgence, Marsala. In
addition to Italian wines there are French, Spanish, German,
Greek, Portuguese, Chilean, Israeli, and domestic wines.

Cedarworkshop

409 Cedar Avenue South, Minneapolis. 336-4147.

Taste, imagination, discrimination, dedication, and
youthful elbow grease — some or all of these qualities are
behind the emergence of many of the shops springing up
in the West Bank area of Minneapolis, near the University
of Minnesota. And to Scott Wilson's and John Kennedy's
Cedarworkshop belongs the whole set of qualities. In addition to their own handmade furniture, they are showing
and selling works of other local craftsmen. Fortunate is
the woodworker, painter, sculptor, or other artist or
craftsman who will have his wares shown off in this tastefully
appointed, uncluttered shop. One beige brick wall forms
an ideal background for a colorful Rya rug, Finnish tapestry,
and wall sculpture; facing this wall, the proprietors chose
to angle unfinished planks of wood for a contrasting texture;
and on the floors bright rugs enhance the effect of each
piece of furniture. It is no surprise that the Cedarworkshop
was chosen by The Minneapolis Committee on Urban Environment as one of ten University-area establishments helping

to lift the face of Minneapolis. The pièce de résistance is perhaps the geodesic chair — a Bucky-Fuller-like dome on fore- and hind-legs. The deep, upholstered interior in a wood frame makes the chair an anti-conversation pit in which to sink, to dream, to withdraw from it all. While somewhat less spectacular than the aforementioned, the proprietors' line of chairs and sofas, outfitted with soft, deep cushions, are sturdy and wonderfully comfortable. Prototypes are on display, but variations on their themes are within reach, to your specifications. Prices are as low as $150 for chairs, $450 for a large couch! Jan Fifield's macramé hangings and chairs are also inexpensive. Paintings and wrought iron sculpture are on display, and Rya rugs can be ordered from catalogues.

Depth of Field

405 Cedar Avenue, Minneapolis. 339-6061.

Although many of its type of wares are to be found here and there in other local stores, this West Bank shop rises above most of its competitors by its consistently high standards of taste. Most noteworthy on its shelves are the varied and useful productions of potters Jeff Oestrich, Ken Olson, Bruce Montgomery, John Coiner, and Anne Goldman. Plates, cups, mugs, vases, bowls, pitchers are in abundant supply and are constantly changing. An extremely inexpensive, appealingly rough-hewn group of bean pots, individual and larger casseroles greet you as you enter, but soon your eye strays to the equally low-priced Japanese vases with the best selection of weeds in town waiting to fill them. Those whose tastes run to prayer rugs will find them at prices ranging from $11 to $20, but even better are the heavy cotton Pakistani bedspreads in a variety of colors at $20 to $25. In a small cookery section you will find *the* right knife for any need, a plethora of pans, and some kitchen esoterica. There is even a specially humidified section which houses plants. While most posters leave us cold, the Friends of the Earth group on display are works of art in themselves. Aesthetically, a small group of photographs outdistances the serigraphs, trendy jewelry, and macrame hangings. But on balance Depth of Field is in the business of outfitting you for the good life.

Dublin Walk

Sheraton-Ritz Hotel, Nicollet Mall between Third and Fourth Streets, Minneapolis. 338-5203.

An excellent source for Donald Davies wool dresses, Waterford crystal, wool ties (conservatives have even been able to find narrow ones there), Irish wool by the yard, shawl scarves, jewelery made of Connemara Marble, Tara china — in short, a really good selection of the best of Irish goods. Prices are not sky high, though of course one is paying for imports, so it isn't a bargain basement either.

The Ethiopian

1407 West Lake Street, Minneapolis. 822-3356.

The Lake-Hennepin area is rapidly becoming a cosmopolitan shopping center, and certainly one of the most "now" clothing shops is this one run by an Ethiopian lady who designs and sews exotic caftans and dashikis in a riot of colors. These are largely in lightweight cottons, but long capes and jacket shirts in heavy homespun cotton are in many ways more intriguing. Some of the gowns are plain with a brilliant decoration on the front. The homespun can be bought by the yard. This shop is well worth a visit by the more daring and might serve as a sartorial shake-up for the less adventurous.

Golden Star Noodle Grocery and Factory

2426 East Twenty-sixth Street, Minneapolis. 721-6677.

As if to carry out the Japanese reputation for understatement, the Golden Star is practically unidentifiable, for an attempt to spell out the name in English with Japanese characters misfired. But it is worth seeking out. (It is on Twenty-sixth Street just east of the point where it is cut off by railroad tracks.) Japanese, Korean, and other Asian specialties abound: prepared seaweed in tins, dried mushrooms, tamari, dried fish resembling minnows, teas, endless tins of mango, canned lychees, seedless longan, grass jelly, pickled radish, canned abalone, boiled gingko nut, large bottles of rice vinegar, various sizes of bottles of soy sauce, sukiyaki sauce, teriyaki sauce. The proprietress keeps fresh fish on hand, but ask for it since it is in a back room. Jammed into one end of the grocery are lacquer bowls, trays, boxes, teapots, sandals, and tabi socks. None of the last group are quite up to the usual high level of Japanese taste, but the grocery is much to be recommended.

India House

Dome City, Fifteenth and University Avenues Southeast, Minneapolis. 331-9121.

On opening day this welcome addition of exotica had a spacious, tastefully appointed display of Indian goods, and we hope that the proprietor continues to leave it as uncluttered. A good selection of the ubiquitous cotton throws is augmented by printed silks and more practical synthetics, as well as scarves in various sizes. Carved sandalwood, ivory, and brass predominate in the decorative arts. In its love of rich detail Indian art is somewhat at variance with the austerity of Western design, so the shop well deserves a visit. Particularly noteworthy are some of the brass pieces, and there is a large selection of jewelry in silver and ivory. The range of foods was not wide in its early days, but undoubtedly has been increased by now. On hand were chenedal beans, cumin seeds, dried and powdered red pepper, sweet neem curry leaves, instant Idli mix, mango pickle in various guises, and mango pulp. Prices were very reasonable.

Ingebretsen's Grocery Store

1603 East Lake Street, Minneapolis. 729-8759.

If you are in the mood for preparing a Scandinavian smorgasbord, an excellent source of supplies is Ingebretsen's Grocery. Norwegian imports predominate, but other Scandinavian countries are well represented. There is a wide-ranging selection of cheeses, including an oddly bland, sweet Norwegian one, Danish Tilsit, Primost, and a host of others. All are priced reasonably. Many versions of herring, a wide variety of Norwegian fish balls, fruit soups packaged for lazy Americans, Swedish caviar, imported glogg mix, Norwegian beers — this will give you an idea of the choices. While Icelandic and Norwegian cod can be purchased frozen, you will probably prefer the fresh salmon, wall-eyed pike, or Canadian crappies. The meat department offers a good sampling of the usual American cuts, but of more interest are homemade liver pâté and mutton roll.

International House of Foods

712 Washington Avenue Southeast, Minneapolis. 331-5691.

Should you need dried seaweed, lotus root, goat milk yogurt, or Philippine milk fish for a special gourmet meal, the International House of Foods will probably have it.

Not all items listed are in stock all of the time, but this is indeed a grocery store which concentrates on imported food. The owner is Chinese, and the House serves the needs of the large Asian student body at the University of Minnesota, but it includes such Middle Eastern foods as halvah, baklava, tinned grape leaves, hoomoos bit tahini, Salonika peppers and olives, and Turkish coffee. In addition there is a wide variety of teas, both English and Oriental. Prices tend to be high, but not too many stores stock cuttle fish in ink, roast eel, squid, braised bamboo shoots, lime pickle, orange flower water, fresh ginger root, and pickled radishes. Some of the supplies needed for cooking Oriental foods are on sale — for example, a handsome Mongolian hot pot in brass for sukiyaki at $35.00, others in aluminum at considerably less. The selection of small lacquer bowls, teapots, cups, and rice bowls shows taste, and cookbooks for Middle Eastern and Far Eastern dishes complete the picture for your Oriental needs. (See our restaurant section for the International House of Foods restaurant and store in Richfield.)

Irish Imports Gift Store

478 Cleveland Avenue South, St. Paul. 690-2125.

This tiny shop is filled with nothing but Irish goods, and while it cannot compete with the Dublin Walk's more glamorous wares, there is more of a country air about its stock of caps, walking sticks, shillelaghs, shawls, wool ties, Galway crystal, place mats, and shamrock china. The jewelry reminds me of Great Aunt Martha's idea of just-the-thing-to-dress-up-a-nice-basic-black, but drop in for a look and perhaps you will come away with the world's best orange marmelade at least.

Kym of Australia

3141 Hennepin Avenue South, Minneapolis. 825-3424.

In a charming old house on Hennepin Avenue, Joan and Kym Knight have set up a very personalized shop specializing largely in Australian imports. The Knights have recreated the homey, unpretentious atmosphere for which the Australians are famous, expressing their own friendliness by serving tea and freshly made Tasmanian tea scones to their customers. The most exotic of their wares are those made by aborigines: boomerangs carved from eucalyptus wood, shields and nulla-nullas (clubs) used in hunting, didgeridoos (musical instruments) painted in earth colors, and aboriginal bark paintings of everyday life and tribal myths. Where else in the Twin Cities would you find a kangaroo pelt or a rug of kangaroo fur for your study? And for your most sybaritic hours buy a couple of white, white deeply piled merino sheepskin rugs which are completely washable and inexpensive at $30.00. Particularly appealing for the younger set are the toy kangaroos, complete with baby in pouch, and while the toy platypuses and wombats are not so attractive they might be a change for some jaded American child. Of course there is a good selection of lovable koala bears, ranging from $4.50 to $26.95 in price. Drawstring fur dilly bags, kangaroo coin purses, kangaroo moccasins, sheepskin coats (washable and made to your measurements), and Australian army slouch hats are all on hand. New Guinean and Fiji imports will soon augment the Australian goods.

Lowell Lundeen

Dinkydale Arcade, 1316 Fourth Street Southeast, Minneapolis. 331-8231.

"Hours, erratic or by appointment." This notice, long seen on the door when Lowell Lundeen was in his old location at 427 Fourteenth Avenue, suggests the casual approach to commerce that he has in his small, interesting shop. Really, in these days of big-daddy-big-mama-super-commercialism, where the retailer's identity all too often gets lost as he anonymously purveys what the manufacturer has already sold on TV, we can only be glad that there are Lundeens among us. For here is a personally selected array of mostly handsome rings, earrings, pins, pendants, and much else, offered by someone who knows and cares about what he is doing. His sources are foreign to some extent (for example, we have bought Middle Eastern jewelry from him) and, in this country, the East and West Coasts especially, because more is happening in jewelry there. Still, potential exists in the Twin Cities, and may be realized and make this an increasingly important center. Lundeen travels to his sources around the country, and keeps in touch as well through catalogs and selections sent to him. The result is an impressive array of conventional through modern work — and no kitsch. The Dinkydale (let's do our best to forget so silly a name) Arcade is a modest but pleasant shopping experiment — with its covered, heated, old-brick-walled row of shops — in an area, Dinkytown, where change comes slowly — and we hope it attracts the clientele that Lundeen's shop there deserves.

Note: Spring has traditionally brought a two-day exhibition and sale of prints and other graphic work at this store, offered by the Ferdinand Roten Galleries of Baltimore. You may want to ask Lundeen to put you on his mailing list, so that you can learn of this and other announcements.

Manuel's Food Market

736 Oakdale Avenue, St. Paul. 225-9555.

In a nondescript, most unbohemian St. Paul neighborhood within two blocks of one another are two grocery stores of very definite character. Down the street from Morgan's (see our separate entry), Manuel's features Spanish and Pan-American groceries. The specialty of the house is Manuel's own chorizo (sausage), but in addition you will find fresh and canned tortillas, many kinds of peppers in jars or cans, Spanish olive oil, enchilada sauce, refried beans, chile con carne, diced cactus, guacamole dip mix, and taco filling.

Middle Earth Art Shop and Gallery

2042 St. Clair Avenue, near Cleveland Avenue, St. Paul. 698-4377.

Ceramics by Dave Frykman et al., bottles, candles, leather handbags and belts, jewelry, photographs, other works of art and craft — there is a feeling of profusion to this shop because of its dimensions (small) and the variety and number of objects for sale (large). But the St. Paul neighborhood is quiet and the atmosphere at the Middle Earth is a congenial one. Visiting it is rather like being in a family-owned country store, but this is not a suggestion of artlessness, for the gathering of pieces here contains many things of interest — for example, a number of ceramic ones — and the nicely understated plain-wood décor is roughly attractive in itself and appropriate for a shop display-ing handcrafts. Except for some incense sticks on sale, all of the merchandise is made by local artists and craftsmen. An odd specialty — at first amusing, though one would soon become bored with it at home — is the gnomelike figures (including a recognizable R. M. Nixon) set in ceramic pieces. The shop is clearly worth visiting, though not at the end of a tiring day, when the interesting objects may not be as perceptible to jaded eyes in the profusion as earlier on.

Moorlane Novelties

2123 Chicago Avenue, Minneapolis. 339-7201.

Although this shop caters primarily to those in search of supplies for large parties, it is a golden source for the modest-birthday-party giver. Prices of small items such as plastic animals and miniature dolls range from 15¢ a dozen up to 80¢ a dozen, but you need not buy a gross or even a dozen of any one thing. The nice thing about Moorlane is that each time one shops there, a certain number of new items show up. Boys will love the goggles with mustaches, play cigars, swords, and compasses, while girls (who probably will also like all of the afore-mentioned) will gravitate toward the charm bracelets, mirrors, purses, and parasols. There is always a good sprinkling of play hats on hand, magnificent balloons that don't give out during the first ten minutes of a party, Japanese lanterns, and Mexican piñatas. When special holidays such as Hallowe'en and Christmas are approaching, you will find an endless supply of inexpensive decorations for those occasions. It is the least expensive way to outfit any affair demanding gew-gaws that won't last long, but must be supplied.

Morgan's Grocery: Lebanese Specialties

736 South Robert Street, St. Paul. 222-9124.

Shed your fried chicken-hamburg-spareribby syndrome and make a trip to Les Morgan's grocery which specializes in Middle Eastern foods. If you are curious enough to eat the many delicious foods of the region, but not sufficiently ambitious to cook them, the Morgans have a number of homemade items awaiting you (and at very reasonable prices). We bought the cooked stuffed vine leaves, lebban (yogurt), hoomoos dip, flat bread, and calamata olives. Our only regret was that we didn't include their raw kibby, baked kibby, and baklava. For the more ambitious shopper who wants to try his own hand at these things, an even wider range of ingredients are available. To name a few, there are feta cheese, vine leaves in jars, pastry leaves for baklava, orange flower water, pomegranate syrup, Egyptian lentils, dry fava beans, gum mastic, kishk, Turkish coffee, ground and cubed lamb. To aid you on your gastronomical plunge are Middle Eastern cookbooks, skewers for shish kebab, and brass coffee pots. Morgan's also stocks a fairly wide range of Mexican foods, including tortillas, taco sauces, and chorizo sausage.

118 East

118 East Twenty-sixth Street, Minneapolis. 825-6000.

When the servantless household became a middle-class reality following World War II, its by-products were a de-emphasis on service plates and multicourse meals and a fortunate switch to tastefully designed, practical dinnerware with an emphasis on informality and good taste which we associate with Scandinavian craftsmen and designers. The owners of 118 East (yes, that is the name of the shop) have culled the best of these arts from all over the world, wisely resisting the temptation to please all tastes, relying instead on their own excellent ones. The result: an artistically arranged, uncluttered shop, focusing largely on the best for the top of the table and the kitchen. The store is vaguely divided into three sections: a retail section houses pottery and earthenware casseroles, plates, crystal glassware, stoneware, vases, Thai chopping blocks, trays, and, for the aficionado whose tea must be brewed to perfect pitch, glass teapots. A second group of similar items reside in the discount section which you will want to luxuriate in, if you appreciate such bargains as Arzberg china at fifty per cent discount, Arabiaware in a variety of stunning and useful pieces, German stoneware, Brazilian rosewood boards, and an everchanging variety of glassware from a number of countries. For your Julia Child days the cookery section will provide the proper baking dish for a quiche Lorraine, the wire whisks all French cookbooks insist on, shells or French porcelain ramekins for a coquille St. Jacques, spring form and other pans not to be found in your neighborhood hardware hangout.

Upstairs at 118 East you will find a fine selection of Marimekko fabrics, Spanish leather goods, and furniture made by the Sawhill furniture company. The restrained pieces on display are notable for their emphasis on clean lines, focusing on the natural beauty of the wood and the leather or canvas coverings. The Sawhill company also sells Creative Playthings furniture.

Pied Piper Children's Shop

1752 Grand Avenue, St. Paul. 699-8877.

The Pied Piper's buyer has obviously proceeded on the assumption that children can learn while playing and need not be gorged with the extravagant foolishness pushed so hard on the telly. However, do not fear that their stock consists of those "educational" toys which please overanxious parents, but which in turn bore the youngsters stiff. It has, among other things, the best stock of Creative

Playthings merchandise in town, but is not limited to that wonderful group of wares. We have long turned to it for one more set of blocks, for a game or a puzzle for any age level, for a multitude of plastic building materials in a variety of shapes, for small wooden villages, and for any number of small and inexpensive but worthwhile presents which one cannot find elsewhere. Raggedy Ann and her brother are usually there in several different sizes. Your junior scientist will enjoy the challenging group of gadgets or a printing press. Although the book section is not large, it too reflects the intelligent care which went into gathering the rest of the merchandise together. Grandparents who have the means and inclination to indulge themselves can consider the farms, castles, and circuses which are in stock at different times. While the Pied Piper is no bargain basement, it is possible to buy very reasonably priced gifts for those years when your child is attending six parties a week. There is also a small but tasteful group of clothes for young children.

A Plethora of Other Shops

The Earth Works Shop at 405 Cedar Avenue, Minneapolis (tel. 339-6061) should be the answer to any weaver's dream, with its stock of looms, spinning wheels, hand-weaving yarns, macramé yarns, craft books, etc. This surely must be the most complete selection of weaving and knitting materials in the cities. In addition, there is an interesting supply of beads and wax dyes for candle dipping. Scheduled to open in the basement of Earth Works in the late autumn of 1972 is John Coiner's gallery, where his fine, inexpensive pottery will be sold.

A few blocks away from Earth Works is the Funk and Rose Leather Company at 212 Fifteenth Avenue South,

Minneapolis (tel. 333-1771), a most ''now'' shop in both its appearance and its wares. At the time of our visit, four local craftsmen were displaying their handmade leather goods, which included a wide choice of handbags, belts, vests, skirts, pants, jackets, chairs.

In a somewhat less Greenwich Villagy atmosphere, but with its own air of individuality, the Woodhouse at 12 Twenty-seventh Avenue Southeast, Minneapolis (tel. 336-2733) is run by the Garmers family, who have on hand the work of some local artisans such as potter Ken Olson, but have in addition very imaginatively turned to the work of craftsmen from the American South, whose art is not often found locally. The handmade wooden bowls, trays, candlesticks, etc. made at Berea College in Kentucky and the covered pitchers, vases, bowls, and other pieces made by a Georgian potter should be singled out for their fine antique simplicity. Ask about these last items should you visit the Woodhouse, for the size of the store prevents all of the items from being displayed at the same time. Other more expectable but tasteful items such as wrought iron candlesticks are on hand.

Pioneer Sausage Company

616 Rice Street, St. Paul. 224-0484.

With the American supermarket invading Europe as the supermarché and supermercato, it is pleasing to note the survival in the U.S.A. of some specialized food shops, of which the Pioneer Sausage Company is an example. In one moderate-sized salesroom there are here offered approximately forty types of lunchmeat and sausage, perhaps twenty fresh meats, around ten smoked meats, and seven canned ham and meat products. There are oxtail, headcheese, double-smoked salami, bratwurst, blood sausage, fresh loin chops, ad nearly infinitum. Prices are reasonable and business on the Saturday afternoon we dropped in was brisk.

Raess Quality Store

1783 St. Clair Avenue, St. Paul. 699-1358.

The last time we were in a *French* French grocery store it struck us that the lines are becoming more blurred every day, for although it would have been dwarfed by the Red Owl, it most certainly was as sterile, efficient and de-individualized. Now it seems that if you want a taste of a provincial, earlier twentieth-century French grocery — · admittedly representing about forty specialty shops in one — you can step into the Raess ladies' emporium, a jumbled, unwell-lighted place with lace curtains at the window. These Alsatian twins have jammed (the operative word here) America, France, the British Isles, Belgium, and many other nations into a 1930's style grocery. But be patient and you will be able to locate goose liver pâté with Perigord truffles in tins large enough for an aficionado (not the usual cracker-and-a-half sample sponsored by gourmet shops), *real* Dijon mustard, escargots, French bread and croissants flown from Paris twice a week, French artichoke bottoms, vine leaves, and a nice spread of English and Scottish jams. It is worth a visit.

Scandia Imports

33 South Eighth Street, Minneapolis. 339-6339.

This is one of the more promising Scandinavian shops in the Twin Cities, with a definite leaning toward Norwegian imports. A beautiful selection of handknit sweaters runs from $16.95 to $29.95 for children, and they are around $49.00 for adults. The rosemaling vams are about $50.00. Knitted caps and mittens, clogs, pewter vases, and candlesticks are in abundance. A wide selection of Scandinavian jewelry turns up a Norwegian specialty called silver solja — a bit on the fussy side, but worth looking at. The Danish and Finnish bronze and silver jewelry are more to our taste and the prices for it are quite reasonable. Don't overlook the handmolded pewter buttons from old Norwegian designs.

Smith's Leather Shop

422 Cedar Avenue, Minneapolis.

Slowly, slowly, but surely the West Bank is turning up some interesting stores, and Smith's Leather Shop, which sells leather supplies as well as handmade leather goods, is one of the more promising. Leather caps, jackets, trousers, belts, and handbags are all crowded into this two-person-wide store. The trousers are in the neighborhood of $70, belts start at about $10, jackets are apt to exceed $100. The largest array of variables is in belts, with a remarkable range of buckles and widths of belt offered.

Swedish Gift Shop

98 South 11th Street, Minneapolis. 335-6123.

This small shop runs a bit too much to wooden animals and trolls for our taste, but there are good glass vases in a variety of colors from $3.50 up. Best of all are the Norwegian copper teakettles at $20.00, and the colorful coffeepots are worth consideration. Also in stock is a group of the aluminum dishes with colorful enamel baked on.

Ukrainian Gift Shop

2422 Central Avenue Northeast, Minneapolis. 788-2545.

This unpretentious shop is best known for its Ukrainian easter eggs, which can be purchased in traditional styles at prices ranging from $1.25 to $5.00. For those who wish to learn the art of decorating them, there are demonstrations before Easter and one can purchase printed information on it. Otherwise, the store is a mélange of somewhat interesting Russian and Eastern European works and inexpensive junk from everywhere. A section of dolls from many countries would please a collector; Ukrainian vases painted in traditional designs are not seen everywhere, nor are you apt to find Ukrainian cookbooks at all book shops. But to sort out the goodies, be ready to wade through piles of button-down sweaters and wool scarves meant to last a lifetime and to ward off East European winters, not for strolling on Nicollet Mall with a warm cocktail lounge in view.

United Nations Gift Shop

55 South Eighth Street, Minneapolis. 333-2824.

Almost avoiding the junky overtones of most such emporia, this small shop should be visited for its carefully selected range of items, some from countries rarely represented in other stores. The most outstanding things we saw were the Thai hand-rubbed temple rubbings on rice paper, running from $4.00 to $8.00. Italian antique-finish wooden trays, jewelry from Greece, England, Thailand, and Nepal, Unicef greeting cards, a United Nations cookbook, and a charming book of children's paintings and poems are among the many possible purchases.

Museums and Art Galleries

This section includes not only institutions and shops devoted to the arts, but museums of various other stamps as well, including the historical and the scientific.

1-4 $1.00   25¢

American Swedish Institute

2600 Park Avenue South, Minneapolis. ~~335-7621~~.   *871-4907*

A classic American success story explains much about this institution. Swan Turnblad, an emigré at eight from Sweden, became manager and then owner of what grew into the largest Swedish-language newspaper in America, and at the century's turn he set about building this French chateau on Park Avenue. In 1929 it was presented to the American Swedish Institute, together with his collections. It is deserving of a visit as much for the statement it makes as to how Americans-who-made-it dreamt and built around 1900 as for its bodying forth of Swedish culture. The gilded-age aspect is expressed in the dimensions of the home (37 rooms, including a ballroom) and its elegant oak and cherry and other paneling, its florid rococo ceilings, its furnishings and appurtenances (easily the most interesting of which is a large marble washstand in a between-stairs lavatory), and in other elements. The Swedish exhibits — some permanent, some not — range from the historically fascinating but aesthetically disastrous fireplaces of brick covered with decorated porcelainized tile, whose massive dimensions dominate many of the rooms just as they do some Stockholm offices today, to replicas of Swedish provincial homes with antiques, to exhibits of contemporary Scandinavian and American arts and handcrafts. The decorative and useful objects in glass from Orrefors and other firms is mixed in interest but, at its best, very beautiful.

A small Museum Shop has gifts of linen, glass, and metals, and merits a visit — especially for its jewelry and lengths from which place mats can be made. Film programs are offered at the Institute. Music too — but if the Sunday-afternoon musicale of the sort we heard prevails, think twice. A number of the visitors no doubt like the comfortable feeling of a home-cum-museum. Some Swedish-accented English can still be overheard in the corridors there, by the way.

The city's turn-of-the-century and Swedish roots are deserving of a palpable record, and an institution which keeps it is worth a look.

Bell Museum of Natural History

University of Minnesota, Seventeenth and University Avenues Southeast, Minneapolis. 373-2423.

The Museum's research and education programs are always in motion and affect the thinking of scientists and the public in many ways. But what is most apparent to the visitor is the Museum's exhibition aspect, which is bodied forth in a wide variety of exhibits on several floors of its building on the University of Minnesota campus. Here, set against often beautifully painted backgrounds by such artists as the late Francis Lee Jaques, are mounted many animals and birds found in the region. These exhibits rarely change, but they are so professionally and artistically created that occasional visits are worthwhile for zoologically interested families.

Younger members of those families should be sure to run about in the Touch and See Room in a wing of the Museum. There, quite palpably in the sense that they *can* be touched, are heads of a moose, bison, and deer, skeletons of a deer and homo sapiens, a bearskin, bones of other creatures, a stuffed coyote and wolf, assorted stuffed rodents, etc. On your way into or out of the Touch and See Room notice the tropical plants in a narrow indoor courtyard. If you're lucky the Museum may happen to turn on the heavy sprinkler to water the plants below. The effect of the water on the leaves and rich earth is exactly, in sight and fragrance, that of a tropical rainshower.

The Museum sometimes offers film programs and lectures, information on which can be obtained from its offices, and there is a bookstore with books on nature just off its lobby on the main floor.

Hennepin County Historical Society and Museum
2303 Third Avenue South, Minneapolis. 332-1814.

The building which houses the museum is quite mentionable, for, though its exterior is somewhat unprepossessing, the interior (when abstracted in the mind's eye from the early Middle Americana on display) is seen to consist of a number of well-proportioned rooms with interesting woodwork and windows and other details, essentially in the Elizabethan manner. This home was planned by an industrialist named George H. Christian, and later became the property of the Society, which is devoted to an understanding of the early settlers of Hennepin County. As a museum, it has rather a crammed look, but that *does* permit a remarkable amount of early furniture, implements, books, china, silverware, bicycles, glassware — the list is virtually endless — to be displayed, grouped according to nature in kitchen, dining room, school room, country store and post office, blacksmith shop, and other rooms. The second floor includes a number of Indian artifacts, beadwork, and a birchbark canoe. Children will particularly like the canoe, and also the old school room, which is in the basement and is complete with desks, teacher's dais, and dunce's stool. There is no entrance fee.

Kilbride Art Gallery

3208 Hennepin Avenue, Minneapolis. 825-3434.

We miss the old *K-B Potboiler*, a publication which used to help us through our depressing winters, but are glad to know that the Kilbride Gallery is still in existence at a new location (and one much easier to park near than was the old downtown hangout). The Kilbride has a stable of about ten artists, among them Nancy Forte, Byron Bradley, Robert Kilbride, and David Rattner. Robert Kilbride's plaques (which he calls "kitchen" art) are intriguing pre-Columbian figures on wood, a good buy at $25.00 and deserving of being promoted to the dining room. Nancy Forte's strange little paintings inside embroidery-hoop-type circles are done in Rome. European prints are on sale at reasonable prices, but the best buys are the handthrown Japanese pots of various shapes at very low prices. The gallery is a pleasant place to drop into for its low-pressure salesmanship, and it has a framing service.

Kramer Art Gallery/Artsign St. Paul

507 Wabasha, St. Paul. 222-5574.

This large, attractive gallery sells "paintings, sculpture, graphics by old and modern masters," but probably does its heaviest business in picture framing, restoration, and the sale of art materials. There is a wide selection of "how to'' art books, a vast array of materials, including, for the do-it-yourself framer, odds and ends of mats at less than $1.00, so that the novice can afford to make some mistakes. The Kramer Gallery has one of the largest, most tasteful groups of ceramics in either city, beautifully displayed in a large room accented by a view of a tiny, ivy-covered, geranium-clad courtyard. When we visited it there was a heavy concentration of work by Lee Byong Ung, a young Korean who has studied with Warren MacKenzie. The works of other potters such as Nils Lou and Art Headley were on hand too. James Nelson's welded sculpture is humorous, interesting, and priced within the pocketbook of the modest-means collector. Shows have featured the paintings and lithographs of David Routon and Warren Westerberg's ceramics. Several of Susan Ecker's magnificent still-lifes caught our eye.

La Galerie

1112 Grand Avenue, St. Paul. 225-1088.

This new gallery specializes almost entirely in the work of contemporary French artists, but many of the works have a weirdly derivative quality, one artist's creations looking very much like those of Van Gogh while a number of others are neo-impressionists. There is a heavy concentration of such painters as Richaud, Duteurtre, Cuvailles, and Laurent. But in spite of the déjà vu air, some works are quite lovely, and if nineteenth-century art is your bag, look in. A Dufy gouache topped the price range at about $3,900, but most prices run from two to three figures and some playful Picasso lithographs at $100 are undoubtedly big sellers. The owner has lived in Paris and seems to know the art scene.

Lorraine Cote Studio Gallery

1610-C West Lake Street, Minneapolis. 824-2878.

This small but pleasantly arranged gallery (though the light is poor in one area) is in an increasingly interesting region of Minneapolis, the several blocks spreading out in all four directions from the intersection of Hennepin Avenue and Lake Street, not far from Lake Calhoun. Lorraine Cote's own work is exhibited in her gallery, and includes large oils and watercolors at such prices as $125, $200, $275, and $300, as well as miniatures in watercolor, portraying subjects in nature, at $8 unframed and $15 framed. Other artists have their work there on consignment; one is F. R. Meisch, whose realistic watercolors capture landscapes and cityscapes and are priced at such figures as $250, $300, and $450. Rentals can be inquired about, and classes in painting and drawing are offered.

Martin Gallery

2116 Second Avenue South, Minneapolis. 336-1837.

The Martin Gallery is as interesting for the setting it provides its artists' works as for the works themselves. The red stone of its exterior, that of a mansion for a family of means in the 1880's, is ugly, to be sure, and the tower and crenellations are typical architectural conceits of the near-fin-de-siècle, but the rooms inside are warm in their reddish brown paneling, which outlines painted plaster walls on which well-framed paintings, watercolors, and prints — for example, of Birney Quick, based on a sojourn in Europe, with prices which range on up from $100 or so — are handsomely hung. And the way in which the rooms are deployed, with views of different parts of a once-elegant, still-pleasant neighborhood near the Minneapolis

Institute of Arts, leads one pleasantly on from one to another. Some have fireplaces still intact, one of them with small, beautiful tiles. There is also a Martin Graphic Workshop, where such works as litho drawings are printed. Just as taste is in part smell, art is in part atmosphere, and the Martin Gallery obviously realizes this and reveals, more than could an antiseptic gallery, how the work of art might look in your living room.

Thurs: 12 - 9   12 - 5

Minneapolis Institute of Arts *870 - 3046*

201 East Twenty-fourth Street, Minneapolis. ~~339-7661~~.

The Institute covers, with varying degrees of emphasis, the arts from ancient times to the present. It offers special advantages to those who become dues-paying members, but is open — at no charge for most facilities — to the entire resident and visiting community of the Twin Cities. And, especially on Sundays or during special events or leading exhibitions, it is *used* by that community, or at least the fair-sized portion of it which is not addicted to such features of American life as television and the refereed violence that football and hockey constitute.

Strolling around the Institute's building reminds one how varied its collections really are. Their breadth is quite remarkable for a museum in a metropolitan area of the Twin Cities' size, and they provide at least an introduction to almost any major form of the visual arts. The Institute's fine print collection and superb collection of Renaissance works has been repeatedly cited by national art critics. Other strengths are in its Chinese bronzes and nineteenth-century French paintings. Works that are particularly worth noting either for their fame or for their beauty or energy include (this is a somewhat personal list): Muse from the Tiber, sculpted in marble in Greece in the second century B.C.

and taken to Rome in ancient times; sections of fifth- or sixth-century mosaic floors from northern Syria, near Antioch; El Greco's "Christ Driving the Money Changers from the Temple"; Rembrandt's "Lucrezia"; tall, not over-ornate oak doors of the French Regency period; G. B. Tiepolo's lean, ascetic "Saint Roch," a painting in interesting juxtaposition to G. D. Tiepolo's better-fed and thoughtful "Head of a Philosopher"; Goya's "Self-Portrait with Doctor Arrieta, 1820"; from the year when Europe trembled with revolutions, 1848, two Daumiers, "The Fugitives," a painting showing a bleak procession which makes one think immediately of Vietnam, and below it a bronze relief by him on the same theme; and finally, in a lighter mood, Camille Pissarro's impressionistic "Théâtre Français in the Rain, 1898," in which one can feel the wetness of the grays and tans of the Paris streets.

The Institute has small collections of African and pre-Columbian art and a small gallery usually devoted to photography. The American (i.e. colonial and United States) collections, including not only painting but also several charming eighteenth-century period rooms and Paul Revere's and others' silver, the Chinese-dominated Oriental galleries (where ritual Chinese bronzes may be seen), the three English period rooms, and the Herschel V. Jones Gallery of prints and drawings should all be mentioned. The Institute also houses a number of temporary travelling exhibitions every year and has originated a number of its own. In 1969 "The Past Rediscovered," a survey of the unfashionable as well as the more familiar aspects of nineteenth-century French painting, drew nationwide acclaim. Writing of the Art Deco show of 1971, the first full-length survey of decorative arts of the 1920's and 1930's, art critic Ruth Berenson observed that the Institute had "outguessed its so-called betters."

A Museum Shop offers books, prints, toys, silverware,

jewelry, and other interesting consumer artifacts. The Institute's educational inreach (to its own facilities) includes free gallery tours, and the outreach (taking the museum to the city and elsewhere) numbers such activities as the Inner City Mobile Gallery, a project of the Institute's Department of Mobile Galleries which visits schools, community centers, libraries, churches, and other institutions offering various exhibits.

In September of 1972 the Institute closed for one year for expansion and remodeling designed by Kenzo Tange of Tokyo, and when it reopens, it is unlikely that the community-wide thrust which has attracted blue-jeaned students, fashionably clad suburbanites, American-gothic-like couples, and others will subside. What is more, children can be seen in these precincts, which also suggests that it is not a museum which sees itself as a temple of the arts. It is Everyman's art center, and its existence is an antidote for the beer signs and automobile laundries of the American City.

Minnesota Artists Association Gallery

1012 Marquette Avenue, Minneapolis. 335-4781.

The headquarters for the Minnesota Artists Association, this gallery is cooperatively owned and run by about fifty MAA artists. It includes paintings, prints, ceramics, and sculpture in various media. Styles run from pretty candy-box landscapes to abstract works. The gallery's present quarters are temporary, and it is to be hoped that a permanent location will allow more space to be devoted to individual works, as they were jammed in when we visited. Smaller watercolors in bins are inexpensive and worth a look. While prices on most works tend to be lower than those of many other local galleries, this is a decidedly eclectic collection and it will take you time to sort out your favorites.

Minnesota Historical Society Museum

690 Cedar Street, St. Paul. 296-2151.

One goes in past the columned façade of the building, past the bookstall just inside the entrance, and up to the third floor. (The Society, directed by Russell Fridley, also has a library, a publication program, and other departments on the other floors.) The museum is compact and has exhibits that are informative for children or adults on aspects of Minnesota history ranging from prehistory to the fairly recent past. Our sons headed first for the full-scale replica of a nineteenth-century one-room log cabin and decided that they would like the small loft in it as their bedroom; below the loft is an all-purpose room for cooking, eating, and sleeping; outside is a small yard. Nearby in this exhibit area are cases with old hats, old license plates, and dolls. In another room, beyond the sentinel-like bison at the entrance, are small exhibits showing the earliest human life in Minnesota (which goes back about 11,000 years), the work of archeologists, mound burials, Ojibwa and Dakota life, and the stages of exploration in the area.

Minnesota Museum of Art

Permanent Collection: 305 St. Peter Street, St. Paul. 224-9471.

Temporary Exhibits: St. Paul Arts and Science Center, 30 East Tenth Street, St. Paul. 227-7613.

The Minnesota Museum is now housed in two locations, the new gallery on St. Peter Street providing more space for its permanent collection than it has had in the past, and the changing exhibitions on display in its old quarters in the St. Paul Arts and Science Center. The permanent collection is particularly strong in Oriental art, with a fine group of Oriental robes and textiles. Other emphases are on contemporary drawings, American crafts, Northwest coastal

Indian art, African art, and a small group of pre-Columbian artifacts. Shows have included a much-acclaimed exhibition of Russian art, and a fine group of photographs, drawings, and models of works of art as used by the Ellerbe Architectural firm to weld art and architecture in a neo-medieval manner. To augment its own fine collection of American crafts, the Museum has sponsored, in conjunction with the Renwick Gallery in Washington, an exhibit of five American woodcraftsmen: George Nakashima, Sam Maloof, Arthur Espinet Carpenter, Wendell Castle, and the late Wharton Esherick.

One Hundred and Eighteen, an Art Gallery

1007 Harmon Place, Minneapolis. 336-1336.

In his television series on nineteenth-century art, Kenneth Clark says that no great picture can be completely abstract, but is always a reflection of experience, predicting that people will turn back to what they see. In partial fulfillment of Lord Clark's prophecy, the art gallery which calls itself "One Hundred and Eighteen" was exhibiting a group of twelve post-pop painters when we visited it. The gallery, an ex-Buick showroom, is spacious, well-lit, and just right for these large creations. It is worth noting that anti-representational art grew partly in reaction to the development of photography, which could do it all anyway, and that in turn this generation of artists is turning to photography for certain qualities they seek to inject into their own work. Jerry Ott's nudes painted from a photograph have a musical, misty, eerie quality, while Paul Staiger paints from a photograph for a flat, anti-life depiction of the homes of Hollywood stars. Other interesting artists represented were Barbara Rogers, Harold Gregor, and Keith Rasmussen. Showing how far the pendulum has swung, Harold Gregor's

Illinois Barn series, with its stark, lonely, unpretty rural views, is reminiscent of Edward Hopper. The gallery's basement featured Tom Supensky's "Famous Paintings in Clay," small take-offs of famous works, which are a kind of cross between a child's fold-out valentine, toby jugs, and Lucca Della Robbia glazes. Our favorite was "Pope Paul Watches the Vasectomy Lesson of Dr. Tulp," offered at $275. Other works on sale ranged from $18 to $500. Twenty-five Midwest artists are represented by One Hundred and Eighteen.

Peter M. David Art Gallery
920 Nicollet Avenue (Second Floor), Minneapolis. 339-6389.

This fine newcomer to the growing world of Twin Cities art galleries specializes in prints. We happened on it during a July sale and found a fine group of etchings and engravings, with a heavy concentration of Richard Volpe's lovely snow scenes, woodlands, and views of Big Sur. A certain number of works by foreign artists are in the gallery; particularly noteworthy are those of the Bombay artist Moti. The gallery frequently has one- or two-man shows. In addition to Volpe, Werner Pfeiffer, and David Smila have been shown. Prices are reasonable. Some of the prints on display were framed, but with such impeccable taste that it is hard to see how one could really improve on the framing.

Science Museum and Planetarium
Minneapolis Public Library, 300 Nicollet Mall, Minneapolis. 372-6543.

Though relatively small in scale, the museum and planetarium facilities of the Minneapolis Public Library possess interest for all but the smallest children, and will even show adults things we thought we knew. On the main floor of the Library, in past a pleasant little sales counter with scientific specimens and guides, is the Time and Space Gallery in which we can sense visually the music of the spheres, in this case the interplay of earth, moon, sun, and other elements in stationary exhibits. Note also the excellent cross-sectional view of a volcano in eruption near the front entrance of the Gallery. The Planetarium offers a series of 45-minute shows about which you may wish to inquire; they are presented on some days without charge and on others for a fee of 25¢ per person. And on the basement level of the Library is a potpourri of exhibits. Perhaps the most interesting are the models of the human heart, stomach, brain, skin, and embryology. Hard by are Egyptian mummies, a palpable reminder of mortality, however well preserved. Other exhibits include those of the loon and other birds, an anteater and duckbill platypus, and butterflies. And there are geological and other displays. No one of these groups will take an eager youngster in great depth into a branch of scientific knowledge, but they serve as introductions. And who knows? perhaps they will send children up the stairs, across the hall, and into the library's book collections as a next step.

Adult education programs in certain of the sciences, school field trips, and rock and mineral identification are offered. Telephone for details.

Science Museum of Minnesota

Arts and Science Center, 30 East Tenth Street, St. Paul. 222-6303.

This (as guidebooks say, somewhat portentously) is recommended. In point of fact, one has no hesitation in citing its virtues. Possessed of a fairly large area in the

Arts and Science Center complex, the Science Museum as a result can offer many exhibits. For example, one can pause, before entering, at a hallway case which asks, "What Is an Owl?" and answers. Inside, there are exhibits — some with recorded sound explanations, and all with written information — on ecology (first barren landforms, then plant life, then interacting plant and animal life), microscopes, DNA and human growth and development, eras in the earth's biological history (life in the sea, then on land), and Eskimo, Indian, and other civilizations. There are skeletons or replicas of early animals in the museum, including a stupendous armadillo, and as an adjunct there is a fine triceratops fossil skeleton in the Arts and Science Center lobby.

En route through the Science Museum, one encounters a puppet theater as an alternative approach to understanding. A somewhat unattractive display of an Egyptian pyramid near the entrance is nevertheless informative, and who can resist the replica of the British Museum's Rosetta stone adjoining the pyramid? Its prototype in the B.M. made possible the decipherment of ancient Egyptian writing.

Minnesotans who are ancient of days will recall, less than nostalgically, the *old* Science Museum in its hilltop mansion aft of the State Capitol, where a basement had been converted into the principal exhibit area. Now there is more space, more light and air, and more sophistication (without going beyond reasonable explanations that adult laymen or children can comprehend). The several exhibits at the new Science Museum engage attention esthetically, and, once you are hooked, they inform you.

The Museum Shop, off the lobby of the Arts and Science Center, has scientific materials (for example, small Bausch & Lomb microscopes), a modest selection of books, and handcrafted articles for home and wear. Thus: Guatamalan skirt lengths, Ecuadoran pillow covers, Mexican tinware and bark paintings, Moroccan tote bags. Etc. A pleasant selection, less than astronomically priced.

Smith Park Gallery for Craftsmen

400 Sibley Street, St. Paul. 226-1119.

Do not be put off by the location of this gallery, for the Park Square Court is being refurbished from dowdiness to elegant smartness. On the mezzanine and second floor you will find a gallery where crafts are on display and for sale, under the aegis of two young men who are devoted to the medieval artisan concept that art is to be used. Their displays do justice to the crafts, for they have resisted the temptation to crowd all together. The range is from subdued, more expectable pots to the trendy macramé hangings, to Judy Ononfrio's Charles-Addams-like creations in raku — looking for all the world like domesticated, petrified sea creatures. For the intrepid buyer, in addition to the raku, there are Jean Stamsta's fiber hangings, Max Zulka's pipes, mugs, and someone else's inflated nylon wall hangings. The more staid writers of this book preferred Jeff Oestrich's superb mugs, vases, and dishes, and some of the jewelry by other artists. The taste is eclectic, but there is no danger that the owners will yield to cute-candles and peppy-posters. Approximately every three months the Smith Park sponsors a new show devoted to one or more craftsmen, with Jean Stamsta's fiber show (which received national attention) an early and promising indication of directions.

Stone Flower Crafts Gallery

1694 Grand Avenue, St. Paul. 699-0535.

This crafts gallery had not completed its showrooms when

we visited it in its early weeks, but there is no question that the additional space will mean a multiplication of beautiful objects. The displays are tasteful in the best sense, for backgrounds are there *as* backgrounds, and the owners are not afraid to dedicate a generous amount of space to each work. Stoneware by Nils Lou and Eugene Johnson included pots, vases, mugs, plates. As a contrast to these more conservative items, Robert Tensing's glass work jazzed up the atmosphere a bit with some apparently phallic hydrants and insects writ large. The milky, poetically colored glass vases, although a bit evocative of Victoriana, are actually much better than anything wrought in that era of the nightmare-dowdy. The Stone Flower's wall hangings seem to us among the better ones around town, for the proprietors have allowed their own quiet good taste to take the lead. Also on hand are a particularly sumptuous group of wool pillows woven by New Zealand craftsmen. They are hand-carded and hand-woven and range from subtle browns and beiges to bright blues. Almost everything at the Stone Flower is reasonably priced and nothing is so large that you must purchase an abandoned mansion in order to house it.

Suzanne Kohn Art Gallery

1690 Grand Avenue, St. Paul. 699-0477.

This small gallery deserves looking into. Don't be put off by the tiny front room, for more things are on hand downstairs. On display when we were there was an exhibit of William Saltzman's works. Other well-known artists such as Phyllis Downes Ames, Jim Breuss, Dean Meaker, and Eugene Larkin are represented, and for more conservative tastes Louis Pohl's silk screen birds at $60 are worth a visit. Several superb still lifes by Susan Ecker made our mouths water. The sell is soft, for Mrs. Kohn really knows and cares about art.

University of Minnesota Art Gallery

Northrop Auditorium, University of Minnesota, Minneapolis. 373-3424.

The University's art gallery, as the old saying goes, is two and three flights up for your convenience. Actually, it is shocking that a major university has so little respect for its art gallery that it continues to house it on the third and fourth floors of Northrop Auditorium, making it virtually inaccessible to many people. A further problem is that, at times, a lack of guards necessitates a cutback in hours. Over the years the gallery's small permanent collection has been augmented by a number of distinguished loan exhibitions, from sources as varied as the Guggenheim and the Fogg Museum at Harvard. And in spite of its physical handicaps it has turned its own collection to interesting uses. In one such use, the Hylton Thomas collection of eighteenth-century decorative arts — a group of etchings, drawings, sconces, candlesticks, fans, paintings, furniture — was arranged as one might have viewed them in an elegant drawing room, and one evening the setting was made complete with a concert of eighteenth-century music. There was a partial repeat of this exhibit, organized in conjunction with a course in French eighteenth-century art. The Cuvillies design for a ceiling, the Haberman rococo wall design, the study for a frontispiece of a book, all reflect an era in which every detail of life received its due. But these works, along with a Watteau drawing engraved by Boucher and Pillemont's "Figures in a Courtyard," belong in a room, not in a hallway where they are something to glance at when the concert-goer is bored with intermission conversation. Shunted off to a corner of the fourth floor like a poor relation (indeed the whole gallery receives that treatment) are more items from the Thomas collection, a priceless French commode, a Sèvres vase and Piranesi's

86

"Arch of Gallienus," all neglected because this part of the gallery is seldom open. Other shows have included WPA Graphics, The Artist as Satirist (Hogarth, Goya, Daumier, et al.), Works by New Studio Arts Faculty, Indian Sculpture from the Haghan Collection.

Walker Art Center

Vineland Place, Minneapolis. 377-7500.

A lavender monolith adjoining the Guthrie Theater is the Twin Cities' leading gallery of modern art. Designed by Edward Larabee Barnes, it was elected as one of nine buildings to receive the 1972 Honor Awards of the American Institute of Architects. Indeed, *New York Times* art critic Hilton Kramer has named it "one of the best contemporary exhibition facilities in the world," placing it above the Guggenheim Museum in New York. The Walker's permanent collection is, however, considered by some art critics to focus too much on the most innovative to be a truly representative collection of modern art. Seven large rectangular galleries were designed to accommodate developments in modern art, and three rooftop terraces display open air sculpture. The somewhat grating Kelvinator whiteness is essential for the color, size, and variety of contemporary works. This was particularly evident in an exhibit of work by seven young regional artists, for each work of art could be studied at length without the intrusion of an adjoining work placed too close to it. Such works as Robert Kerns' "Epicalligraph" and Mario Merz's "Spaces and Objects Defined by Placement of Neon Numbers" depended upon the luxurious amounts of space provided in the Walker. In other rooms, more conventional easel paintings of earlier decades, such as a group of Marsden Hartleys and works by Jack Levine, Lyonel Feininger, and Max Weber, received somewhat less royal treatment, but were at least *there*, as was a particularly note-worthy group of Bill Brandt photographs. A Matisse sculpture show was another recent feature.

The Walker has two auditoria, a medium-sized one for concerts and films, and a small one — a purple conversation pit — in which slides can be shown, such as those depicting the seven young artists at work as a preview of their creations. The bookshop, sharing in the prevailing openness of the Walker, is not closed off, but instead forms part of a spacious lobby, with an inviting array of wares. The cafeteria on the top floor carries out the starkness of design pleasantly, as a study in black and white with brilliant paintings at each end, and it overlooks one of the rooftop terraces. The tea, coffee, cookies, sandwiches, etc., are, incidentally, much cheaper and more edible than most cafeteriology.

Sunday is really family day at the Walker, for the many brave young parents who bring the kiddies to view the exhibits can take advantage of the art activities offered for young children, such as a happening with clay and finger painting in which *hands in* is the rule. The Walker hosts a number of other activities, such as film series, concerts, symposia on photography; and the following description would have pleased even the most jaded appetite: "Game for two players: a ritual game for two participants and no audience using musical devices, laser patterns, colored strobes, and films of video synthesis by Morton Subotnick."

West Bank Art Gallery

415 Cedar Avenue, Minneapolis. 332-4963.

The opening show at this new gallery featured a group of University of Minnesota faculty artists, including Vic Cagliotti, Peter Busa, Roger Crowell, and Zig Priede, in the most avant-garde art to be found in the cities in recent months. A somewhat less formidable second show, with work by Freddy Munoz and Diane Williams, followed. And for those with somewhat more timid tastes a group of paintings and woodcuts by Gordon Mortensen were for sale. The woodcuts (extremely reasonably priced) were some of the most interesting Minnesota scenes we have stumbled on in our peregrinations. Good luck to another promising and much needed gallery.

West Lake Gallery

1612 West Lake Street, Minneapolis. 822-0600.

The West Lake's 1972 brochure announces that "there's a new look at the West Lake Gallery — white wall, grey carpeting, excellent lighting, enlarged exhibition space — all to emphasize the Art's the Thing." And this is essentially true. A gallery owned cooperatively by ten artists, the West Lake sponsors twelve exhibitions a year, with a one-man show on the first floor and bins with individual artists' offerings in the cellar, where you will find watercolors, prints, collages, and drawings. The one drawback to this latter group is that although prices are reasonable, the downstairs gallery's wares are already framed and you end by paying for someone else's ideas of proper dressing for your purchase. Among artists represented when we visited were Jo Rollins, Alice Benjamin, Caprice Kueffner, and Verba Weaver. Ron Gallas' fine ceramics were there in abundance. Elaine MacCarthy's show was given plenty of elbow room on the first-floor main exhibition gallery. This is important, as some of her works — the vibrant "Night Street," for example — would suffer if they were jammed into a small gallery. There seemed to be no one school of art represented, and prices won't take your breath away. This is a good gallery for your shopping if you tend to be frightened off by the super-up-to-dateness of some other shops.

Theaters

Our coverage of the theater scene in the Twin Cities, and to a certain extent in their suburbs, has been fairly thorough. It is altogether possible that each new season will see some new groups and that some of those listed will have died aborning, for a number of companies have limped along on not much more than talent and youthful zeal, and, as a result, may never produce another play. And it would be foolish to pretend that all companies and productions are equally good. But many will surely survive, and healthily, for there has been a growth of dramatic creativity in Minneapolis and St. Paul.

In most cases our policy is to be as concrete as possible, within the limits of space of a guidebook intended as a highly portable reference work. To this end, we discuss one particular production which we attended, review its pros and cons, and indicate other plays performed by each group. We have been critical of shortcomings in certain companies, but we see a number of accomplishments and many hopes for the future. It is unfortunately true that audiences still gravitate mostly toward fare which washes lightly over them, avoiding the ''difficult'' but often interesting works which require thought and attention. But we also believe that the pastel period in community theater is, in many ways, coming to an end. The Cricket Theater, which bravely persisted in performing before miniscule audiences for much of their first season, ended that season playing *The Basic Training of Pavlo Hummel* to packed houses. And Tomas MacAnna, artistic director of the Abbey Theater in Dublin, expressed great praise for the talented actors whom he directed in *Borstal Boy* for the Chimera Theater. The Guthrie Theater has, of course, provided a high standard of professionalism and our summary pays this central jewel its due, but it is not a diamond whose light should blind Twin Citians to other theatrical fare.

In March, 1973, the community theaters of Minnesota will hold a festival competition open to all community theaters in the state, from which one winner will go to the regional festival, that winner in turn entering the national competition in Lincoln, Nebraska. From there the national winner will go to an International Theater Association event in Monaco. Whether or not any of the groups discussed here will be chosen even for the first leg of the trip, it should be noted that this is the first time Minnesota theaters have staged their own festival. Perhaps this is symbolic of an increasing assurance, a growing confidence in an art form which is often the most complex and palpably the most human of them all.

Brave New Workshop

2605 Hennepin Avenue South, Minneapolis. 377-2120.

Brave New Workshop Also

1430 Washington Avenue South, Minneapolis. 333-9687.

It's a long way from Vienna, but for more than a decade Dudley Riggs has been helping to fill what would have been a noticeable lacuna in coffee house satire, lampooning local and national institutions and personalities in what are now two Workshops, where different shows run concurrently. Riggs himself is a marvelous impresario. His introductions to some performances are small masterpieces of humor, and he may comment imaginatively and more or less ad libitum on items from an early edition of next morning's newspaper. In recent years the Workshop's reviews have had some of the rough edges of earlier days smoothed out, working them free of some of their more grating amateurish aspects. The reviews we have seen at either location have consisted of a series of skits under such inventive umbrella titles as *The Day the Muzak Stopped* (one hopes the title is prophetic), *Adrift on the Floating Dollar*, and *Overdrawn at the Sperm Bank*. The satire has varied targets — el presidente and his appointees, credit-carditis, Camp Inward Bound, and much else. The cast, apt to be young and wonderfully energetic, has been known to end the evening with an updated version of a stylized Oriental chamber drama as well. Note that one can order food and nonalcoholic beverages to be served at table in the theater. (For a description of the Workshop's restaurant menu, see our restaurant section.) Admission to the theater is $2.75 per person, and season tickets are available to students.

Children's Theater Company of the Minneapolis Institute of Arts

201 East Twenty-fourth Street, Minneapolis. 333-3371.

While American children's theater productions in general have been in the amateur, nice-hobby-for-middle-aged-ladies stage, John Donahue's professionalism has outdistanced practically all other groups, receiving serious attention from critics and large foundation grants. At the 1972 International Congress of Theater for Children and Youth at Albany, New York, the production of *Hang onto Your Head* by the Children's Theater Company under Donahue was recognized as technically the most accomplished work presented, and it stirred up a lively controversy among the delegates for its non-establishment content. Donahue is patently not papering over the problems of growing up, and he is giving a much-needed shot in the arm to theater for young people, both technically and in content. When we attended a performance of *The Cookie Jar* in March of 1972, the Company was still playing in the old Institute auditorium, with its tiny stage and poor sight lines. The new theater to be built as part of the over-all expansion of the Institute will give Donahue opportunities to demonstrate his abilities further as director of productions for children and adults. (See the entry in this section for adult productions of the Children's Theater Company.)

The Cookie Jar, which he wrote, directed, and produced, is aimed at children of ten or older, but it was also enjoyed by a seven-year-old, who could follow it with the assistance of whispered explanations by a parent. It is a musical with a moral for our pampered, acquisitive offspring; a quest for the recipe for the good life by a return to giving rather than by a push toward getting. A white boy and a black girl feel lost in a world where everyone is playing one-up-manship and it is easier to grab than to give. Even more insidious than the warring street gangs and racist groups are a poisonous body of adults, the Stale Cake Company — TV barkers writ large who urge one and all to "get, get, get," meanwhile snarling at the kids. After Mother Mary helps the boy and girl to find the lost recipe for living, a huge cookie is served to the grabbers, and then there are cookies for members of the audience. A delightful mélange of dance, jazz, blues, and spirituals is interspersed with the action, and the costuming — in part a reflection of the shoddy-successful materialism of our world — is marvelous. The whole effect is an antidote to

the boob-tube commercialism that has laid waste so many of television's possibilities in this country. The Children's Theater Company cast is able to give a sense of talking directly to the audience without being cloying or excessively preachy.

While this play is aimed at the older child, others have been suitable for younger children: *Peter and the Wolf, The Ugly Duckling, Hansel and Gretel, Robin Hood, Sleeping Beauty,* and *Madeline and the Gypsies,* for example. Admission for individual tickets has been $1.75 for children, and $2.50 for adults, and there are special rates for school groups. Telephone the Company for information about its performance schedule, and about the place of performances during the construction interim at the Institute.

Adult Productions of Children's Theatre Company of the Minneapolis Institute of Arts

201 East Twenty-fourth Street, Minneapolis. 333-3371.

Artistic director John Donahue's widening reputation in the world of children's theater should not obscure the fine productions of this company for adults, epitomized by a sparkling version of Sheridan's *The School for Scandal* in 1972, presented in cooperation with the College of St. Catherine. A 750-seat theater for the Company, with rehearsal rooms, education areas, and production shops, is under construction as part of the Institute's expansion program. Meanwhile, this very professional group brought alive, on a postage-stamp-size stage in the Institute's old auditorium, Sheridan's eighteenth-century upper-class world of gossip, intrigues, and assignations, where virtue has not become so repulsively pure as it was to do in the following century. Joseph Surface, one of literature's archetypal hypocrites, was happily not overdrawn by Richard

Ashford, and instead was seen as a convincing, timeless social operator. Elizabeth Keagy as Lady Teazle and Richard Ramos as Sir Peter managed the verbal duelling scene beautifully, while the cast was remarkable for its choreography in the famous scene in which characters are concealed by screens. Singling out highlights, however, is not meant to put down the production as a whole; it was lively and polished, the costumes were handsome, and Hiram Titus's music was enchanting.

Other adult productions in 1971-72 were in a new series, Le Petit Théâtre, which included *Spoon River Anthology, The Sitwells at Sea, Variations on a Similar Theme*, and *An Evening of Leonard Cohen*.

See also the entry for the children's productions of the Company.

Chimera Theater

Crawford Livingston Theater, St. Paul Arts and Science Center, Tenth and Cedar Streets, St. Paul. 222-0792.

A relative newcomer to the burgeoning theater world of the Twin Cities, the Chimera Theater shows that there is always room for one more of real quality. While the Crawford Livingston Theater seems a down-at-heels but respectable relation of its more glamorous cousin Guthrie, the quality of its productions is not constrained by its appearance. And this was particularly true of Brendan Behan's *Borstal Boy*, directed by Tomas MacAnna, who has been artistic director of the Abbey Theater, Dublin. Frank MacMahon's adaptation of Behan's autobiography sets up a counterpoint between the idealistic though lippy adolescent arrested as an IRA agent at age sixteen and the older gone-to-seed Behan. Without preaching, the play is a telling indictment of prison life and the vicious circle of violence.

In fact, the humor and violence so inextricably interwoven here might well be a symbol of Ireland's history. MacAnna's reliance on song epitomized both the camaraderie and endurance of youth. He enhanced his directing with his own set designs, using lighting to convey prison, church, etc. Al P. Johnson as young Behan moved from a convincingly brash tabula rasa to a more canny borstal boy, while Victor Pinhiero retained the poetry in the barfly that Behan became. MacAnna was particularly fortunate in having in the Chimera Theater a group of actors who could convey the humor and horror of the halfway house represented by borstal life. Other Chimera productions include Strindberg's *Miss Julie*, Peter Shaffer's *The Royal Hunt of the Sun,* Molière's *The Imaginary Invalid,* Leroy Jones' *Dutchman*, Pirandello's *Six Characters in Search of an Author*, and, for children, *The Emperor's New Clothes*.

Cricket Theatre

345 Thirteenth Avenue Northeast, Minneapolis. 333-1411.

The façade and the seating area for the audience are as they must have been when this company's building functioned as a neighborhood movie palace. But there has been a last motion picture, and now one finds at Bill Semans' Cricket Theatre a large thrust stage on which are offered such plays as *Dracula*, Gary Munn's *The Judas Applause*, and David Rabe's *The Basic Training of Pavlo Hummel*, an antiwar play. We saw *The Judas Applause*, which seeks through present action in a Washington saloon in April, 1865, and through flashbacks to his childhood to account for John Wilkes Booth's motivation in murdering Lincoln, and (by extension, in a slightly contrived ending) the motivation for John F. Kennedy's assassination. Munn locates the answer essentially in Booth's idée fixe — that he must be more prominently remembered by history than his over-bearing father, the actor Junius Brutus Booth — and in John Wilkes' uneasy realization that his father was the better of the two of them, despite Junius's flights of madness. David Ode's direction moved the audience's attention nicely back and forth over the stage, and over time as it was perceived in John Wilkes' mind — with lighting, music, and sets being used adroitly. The cast was uneven in its abilities, but among the very convincing performers were the two principals, Budge Threlkeld acting John Wilkes in the overblown manner of the mid-nineteenth-century stage, and Clive Rosengren as a Junius Brutus with a superb range of expression and with a large frame which suggested the larger-than-life aspect he had in his son's mind. The company's costumes were all fine, by the way, including Junius's long underwear, worn as he greets the sun with cockcrows in a flashback. One must also note the play's overture, as it were: songs of the period played before the performance began by two singers who accompanied themselves on banjo and guitar; this led into the guitarist's song of Booth, which set the stage for the action of the play.

Edyth Bush Theater of Hamline University

690 Cleveland Avenue South, St. Paul. 699-1337.

One should not be misled by the inward and outward appearance of this company's building, for the company itself and the choice of plays have some genuine interest. Let us get the building out of the way by saying that it resembles nothing so much as a small-town movie theater of the 1930's, with high ceiling, drably colored walls and seats, and a big proscenium stage. A nice touch is the serving of free entr'acte coffee in a lounge belowstairs, but on the evening in question the lounge was hung mostly with paintings of the sort that motels appear to purchase by the gross.

Still, the play's the thing to catch our conscience, and we saw at the Edyth Bush a fascinating performance of *In White America*. This is a play for reader's theater, and in this case parts were read from open looseleaf binders by actors seated on stools on the crescent-shaped forestage, with the rear of the stage curtained off. There are ample opportunity for vocal expression and a minimum of physical action. This approach well suits the material used by playwright Martin Dubermann, a Princeton historian, which was a variety of very moving documents — speeches, diaries, court records, memoirs — on the position of the black in American history from the time of the slave trade to Little Rock, Arkansas in 1957. The company, consisting of middle-aged and younger actors and actresses, was well-directed and -rehearsed, and (though one member overacted) quite competent on the whole, with some parts being done remarkably well. The cast was abetted by two folksingers with guitars, whose songs were effectively interspersed with the chronologically arranged readings.

Other plays offered by the Edyth Bush company have included Samuel Beckett's by-now-classic tragi-comedy *Waiting for Godot*, Emlyn Williams' drama of suspense *Night Must Fall*, and James Thurber's *Thurber Carnival*.

Guthrie Theater

725 Vineland Place, Minneapolis. 377-2224.

This is of course the leading company in the Twin Cities, and one of the ornaments of regional professional theaters in the United States — though, like many artistic endeavors, it has shone steadily in some years and with a fitful light in others. It is enjoying another of its successful eras now, under the artistic direction of Michael Langham, who came to Minneapolis after directing the Stratford Festival Theatre in Ontario, and vivacity, color, movement, excellent timing, and good casting have been hallmarks of the company's productions at the Guthrie Theater, which adjoins the new Walker Art Center. The season runs from July into the winter, and on a summer evening especially the lively play of light and glass and concrete of the theater building suggests the movement inside, where the thrust stage with its several levels offers many fine juxtapositions for the actors and actresses, gives audiences the palpable proximity of the cast, and (except for some seats back under the balcony) allows the lines to be heard as they should. The vibrant design of the interior adds to the sense of *theater* — of the stage as a heightening of, and not realistically identical to, life. (The Guthrie Theater as architecture is discussed in our section devoted to architecture.)

The repertoire consists mostly of classics from ancient Greece, Europe, and America, sometimes in adaptations, sometimes with costuming from another period. The choices are often good, occasionally inexplicable. (Why was Eugene O'Neill represented first by a thin group of sea dramas? But the error was later redeemed by so splendid a play as his *Touch of the Poet* with Robert Pastene in the leading role.) And there is one glaring omission, for there has been nothing from Ireland, though Sean O'Casey or Brendan Behan would seem to offer lively possibilities from that direction. Still, there is much to be thankful for. Take Anthony Burgess's adaptation of Rostand's *Cyrano de Bergerac*, directed by Langham in 1971 at the Guthrie, with Paul Hecht in the title role. The production moved beautifully back and forth between great vigor and bittersweet serenity, as Burgess, Langham, and Hecht brought out the idea of panache — of behaving with assured style even when one is losing or is ridiculous. The 1972 season shows how long a bow the company draws in types and periods of drama: *A Midsummer Night's Dream*, Steinbeck's *Of Mice and Men*, Sir John Vanbrugh's *The Relapse, or Virtue in Danger*, an overlong but quintessentially satirical Restoration comedy with a splendid Lord Foppington by Bernard Behrens, Eugene Labiche and Marc-Michel's *Italian Straw Hat*, and the world premiere of a new translation and adaptation by Burgess of Sophocles' *Oedipus the King*, in which Burgess with strong imagery shows the unwitting and finally conscious way in which Oedipus becomes the instrument of his own destruction, and yet in his agony saves the city of Thebes.

A core of cast members has remained with the company for many years, most notably the versatile Pastene. Other actresses and actors have come for a play or a season or two and moved on. With rare exceptions they have worked well together and not sought to upstage each other. These factors and the others we have cited have kept even the occasionally weak plays from being devoid of interest — and the successes have usually been stunning ones.

Various types of season tickets are available (consult the Theater for details and prices), and it is well to telephone in advance when booking seats for a single play.

Footnotes: A Guthrie touring company, returning also to Minneapolis for several performances, has done *Fables Now and Then* under David Feldshuh's direction; and the Stratford Company has come down from Canada and played for a few weeks in late winter on the Guthrie's boards (its greatest achievement here being Webster's *The Duchess of Malfi*).

Lakeshore Players

Corner, Sixth and Stewart Streets, White Bear Lake. 429-5674.

Once upon a time the theater was a place of entertainment and often, as a side dish, one's mind and emotions were stretched, so that as with any work of art, the onlooker's perceptions were enlarged. The trend nowadays seems to be about three steps backward to the medieval miracle plays produced to instruct the illiterate in Biblical lore. *Ravaillac* is one of a burgeoning body of dramatic fare for the modern illiterate, hitting him over the head with nonverbal banalities, a rock version of a seventeenth-century assassination which was in addition intended to mirror the murder of a young man escaping Czechoslovakia in the 1960's. The program notes state that "the connection between this event in seventeenth century French history and the death of Cathala's friend is not readily apparent. . . ." We'll buy that. Having given up dialogue beyond a few woodenly worded and equally stiffly delivered lines, the production resorted to messages flashed on a screen. A cast who could not dance — nay, even *move* gracefully — shuffled about in ill-fitting winter longies. (Get it? It's Everyman.) The hero-martyr Ravaillac is of course the King's fool (another brand new piece of irony). The Lakeshore Players have offered a more promising *Man for All Seasons*, and have done *Man of La Mancha, As You Like It, Plaza Suite, and Camelot,* so perhaps *Ravaillac* represented a bit of midsummer madness!

Mill City Theater Factory

2746 Stevens Avenue South, Minneapolis. 823-3534.

This group, the former Alive and Trucking Theater, has as its rationale the belief that theater must be involved in a dedication to causes of the common people. Its original play *The People Are a River*, which used records of the Indians, settlers, and workers in Minnesota history, had behind it a good idea. Unfortunately, good notions and right causes do not a work of art make — and what emerged

proved to be a less than gripping dramatization of history. Heavy-handed enactments of prehistoric geological eruptions were quite unconvincing; the narrator was given impossibly bad poetry, and her own "elocutionary" style did nothing to improve on it; the depiction of a turn-of-the-century laborer resorting to drink after his exhausting and mind-flattening work was so overdrawn that we guffawed; the nicey-nice farmers were incredible in their one-dimensionality. It must be said that the music was exceptionally good, and that one actress showed real promise, but, alas, in most cases the combination of non-theater with non-acting added up to a non-event.

Minnesota Ensemble Theater

3104 Sixteenth Avenue South, Minneapolis. 722-5479.

The most avant-garde of the local theater companies, MET has the brashness to take on the difficult experimental dramatic fare which we associate with the Provincetown Players of the early twentieth century and the Firehouse Theater of the 1960's; for this is drama which is too often sidestepped by the more comfortably established groups. MET's success is largely due to a company of unusually tenacious and loyal young actors and actresses, and director Joe Walsh, rather than to a cushy endowment. During the winter of '72 the cast was willing to hitchhike to rehearsals in order to pull together Mike Green's *Children*, a play written especially for the company. Other recent productions have included R. D. Laing's *Knots*, Chekhov's *The Seagull*, and T. S. Eliot's *Murder in the Cathedral*. The last, which was also videotaped by Herb Grika of the Minneapolis College of Art and Design and Bill Tift of Communitube for educational uses, exemplifies the group's willingness to put some new clothing on a challenging, not always successful poetic drama. Eliot's decision to use the verse of *Everyman* poses a metrical problem for any group and

may account for Walsh's choice of a West Indian setting
to evoke the essence of the early Christian church. The
audience was greeted with a voodoo drum, West Indian
dancing, and a remarkably bloodless person who hung
upside down overhead. While the dancers were excellent,
their delivery of lines was often monotonous, and the
themes — one being the analogy between Thomas á Bec-
ket's temptation and Christ's temptation in the desert, and
another the power struggle between church and
state — were at times smudged by the too seductive dancing
and drums. A very positive quality of the group, its seem-
ingly boundless energy, is too much for the size of the
small church building in which they perform. But for their
willingness to take on difficult and/or new plays, often by
unknown playwrights, their persistence in eschewing the
stale and safe middle of the road, MET is to be commended
and no doubt will in time learn to adjust their style to the
size of the theater. MET also sponsors poetry readings.

Old Log Theater

County Road 82, Excelsior. 474-5951.

The Old Log is one of the more firmly established
community theaters and a most enviable plant it has, with
a spacious theater building, where drinks and light suppers
are served before performances, and a separate scene
shop — all set in lovely grounds, not a bad place to
be on a summer evening. And the Great Grey Way,
firmly in the middle of the road, is unquestionably the
safest place to be in the theatrical world, for the menu
of *dramatic* fare is standard summer stock, as safely blue
chip as its audience seems to be. It is sad that in such promising surroundings one is offered such slush as Neil Simon's
The Last of the Red Hot Lovers (advertised as "adult entertainment" — we question that). It is a situation comedy
worthy of a grade of "C" from the not very selective

television ratings. As for the acting, Ken Senn, an amusing Zero Mostelish type somewhat miscast in the role of Barney Cashman, did manage to bring the right amount of uneasy oafishness to the role of a happily married, middle-aged dullard whose ponderings on the brevity of it all have led him to attempt an affaire de coeur. While the ladies were uneven in their roles, all were professional actors who should have been given a chance to try something with at least genuine humor in it. Other recent offerings have included *Forty Carats, How the Other Half Loves, See How They Run*. Prices for tickets are $3.00 and group rates are available.

Peppermint Tent Theater

University of Minnesota Theater, Scott Hall Ticket Office, Minneapolis. 373-2337.

The red and white striped Peppermint Tent has been lodged next to the University's Showboat for a number of years, offering up delightful confections-with-a-bite for children. A performance of James Thurber's *Thirteen Clocks* was filled with action, and often action which elicited the audience's involvement. The villain, a semi-comic, scary creature on one roller skate, continually tried to pry from his young audience word of the whereabouts of the ingenuous young minstrel come to start the thirteen clocks and set free the inevitable captive princess, Sara Linda. Costumes were bright, dialogue short, and, best of all, our literal-minded TV kiddies were required to stretch their imaginations a bit. They saw how successfully the actors could simulate clocks (all making different sounds), bridges, furniture, thunder, lightning, and trees. All of this was interspersed with much singing and dancing.

Note: The seating is on backless benches and you should

arrive fifteen minutes before starting time, as it is on a first-come-first-served basis, but, to keep squirmability in check, orange drinks and crackerjack are available for ten cents each. Other offerings have included Carl Sandburg's *Rootabaga Stories*. The season runs from early June through August. Prices: Individuals, $1.00, groups of twenty-five or more, .60 apiece.

Rostopov Puppet Theater

Brave New Workshop, 2695 Hennepin Avenue South, Minneapolis. 377-2120 or 333-9687.

Bill Eden has created the most imaginative puppets we have ever seen, larger than the usual dolls, and he manipulates them all and enacts all of the parts very professionally, in a loosely organized production which skillfully draws the young members of the audience into his show. For the three Ervins attending the favorite was the dopey but lovable Roger Silly, the pianist who had lost his piano (''a Steinway-rooney''). Roger's purple fright wig and yellow suit were most engaging, but the impresario, Walter the Worm, ran him a close second in appeal, sporting a red mop of a head that doubled in brass, mopping the stage. Other characters were the befuddled theater owner who has lost his show, Mr. Rostopov, a nineteenth-century lady opera singer and the somewhat frightening (but in a deliciously shivery way, not enough to send anyone home to nightmares) Magda the Gypsy Lady. The humor was somewhat beyond a seven-year-old at times, but on the whole had a broad enough range for a five- to twelve-year-old group. The Workshop's smallish room is fine for this kind of production. Hot chocolate, capuccino, cider, coffee, and cakes are served at table during performances, but one is not under any pressure to buy. The price of admission to the puppet show is $1.00 for children, $2.00 for adults, and well worth it.

Shakespeare in the Streets

P.O. Box 14192, Minneapolis 55414.

In the past decade the trend in all of the performing arts has been to remove the "noli me tangere" wrappings, to rid art of its rarified atmosphere, one which has undoubtedly scared off many potential viewers. One of the most delightful local manifestations of this trend is the Shakespeare in the Streets company, which has, so to speak, taken the Bard out of the theater and put him back where he belongs, with the people. A small, easily portable stage, with red and gold backdrops and pennants flying, is set up out of doors in a number of locations around the Twin Cities, making it possible for a diverse group of citizens to view the plays without the necessity of driving long distances. Further, the performances are free, with donations being appreciated but not by any means extracted. A relaxed atmosphere is enhanced by an initial half hour of singing of a mixed bag of songs ranging from Simon and Garfunkel to Elizabethan lyrics such as "Joan, Come Kiss Me Now."

But the play's the thing. The group wisely chose three comedies for the 1972 season, and the one we attended, *Twelfth Night*, was given an exceedingly broad interpretation (necessitated in part by competition with noise pollution, courtesy of various passing gasoline-powered atrocities). The bawdier, earthier aspects of Shakespeare were very much underscored — but, after all, the boys in the pit did not read *Twelfth Night* in a literature class, they went to see it as an afternoon's relaxation. The S.I.T.S. company evokes something of such an afternoon at the Globe, circa 1600.

The hamminess of the mistaken identity on which the plot depends is somewhat grating when one sits in a theater built for audiences of the 1970's, but this wears well out of doors. With the exception of a badly played Duke Orsino, the cast ran from fair to delightful. The last epithet is particularly applicable to Malvolio — here is just the right amount of foolish sanctimoniousness and general dopiness, so that when he is undone in the love scene with Olivia we are torn between laughter and tears. Running Malvolio a close second is a charming Feste. Maria, Sir Andrew Aguecheek, and Sir Toby Belch are slapped out with the broadest of strokes, but the timing is wonderful. Much is made of the physical aspects of the play, so that the gymnastics make up for what some of the audience may not have been able to hear. And the many children in the audience were rapt — one young lady, who is on the right side of six and a half years, walking back and forth in front of the stage, entranced, for two hours. All of this is a much better introduction to a Shakespeare comedy than some Professor Dullsville's disquisitions on the niceties of Elizabethan punning and syntax.

Consult newspapers for times and places.

Stagecoach Players

Highway 101 between Savage and Shakopee. 825-4225.

The playbill for a production of *After Dark* by the Stagecoach Players announces "*After Dark* by Mr. Dion Boucicault, adapted by Mr. Lee Adey, Cast of Characters (in order of their glorious appearance)." The portentous formality of a nineteenth-century theater program is warmly evoked in this quintessence of Victorian heavy-handedness. With the tinkling piano telling the audience how to react and just the right amount of overacting, the Stagecoach

Players are a delight to eye and ear. Villains who manipulate lost heirs, faithful preliberation wives who attempt the leap from the bridge rather then be a burden to hubby, former Oxonians on skid row — you name it, it's all there. And inbetween the ridiculously brief scenes are sandwiched olios, ranging from a lovable spoofing of Fred Astaire back to can-can tootsies. A Sunday afternoon audience was composed largely of families, and every age group seemed to be enjoying it. Unreconstructed nostalgiacs of any age will want to allow some time to walk through Sand Burr Gulch at the back of the theater. (See description of the Gulch in our miscellaneous section.)

Theater in the Round

245 Cedar Avenue, Minneapolis, near West Bank Campus of University. 336-9123.

The company's work is suggested by its production of Arthur Kopit's *Indians.* As directed by Scott McCoy, the somewhat overdrawn Wild West atmosphere of the performance underscored the place of any minority in American life: not just exploitation in the more obvious senses, but the degradation that results from being treated as an exhibit in a sideshow. For this reason the casting of a black in the part of Sitting Bull was justified; he universalizes the issue. Buffalo Bill as played by Richard Jackson was marvelous, summing up in his personality the unthinking manner in which America has drifted into these problems.

The theater is small, truly a theater in the round, with few possibilities for scenery. The effective use of lights in one sequence of *Indians* suggested a nickelodeon, and evoked a turn-of-the-century form of entertainment, enhancing the feeling of unreality and of fragmentation in an America where Indians became freaks in a Wild West show.

The sight lines from our seats were fine, but we could not always hear the players.

Theater in the Round celebrated its twentieth anniversary in 1971–72 with a vital, varied program. In addition to *Indians*, the group produced *The Boys in the Band*, *The Iceman Cometh*, *The Women*, *Pygmalion*, *Cock a Doodle Dandy*. Auditions were open to everyone. For $2.00 plus a season ticket you can become a member, and anyone can apply to work backstage or as an usher, pushing soft drinks.

Theater 1900

Howard Conn Fine Arts Center, Plymouth Congregational Church, 1900 Nicollet Avenue, Minneapolis. Tel. 339-6317.

The curved proscenium stage, brick walls, and tweedy warm-beige seats of the theater are esthetically pleasing, but we wondered about the acoustics, for important lines sometimes were blurred when spoken on the stage. But the moderate size of the theater was ideal for the intensity of *Woyzeck*. David Ball translated, adapted, and directed this moving fragment left by the twenty-three-year-old German physician Georg Büchner in the 1830's.

The fragmentary aspect reinforces soldier Woyzeck's fragmented sense of a reality which becomes increasingly painful to him, and John Martin's rendition of the central role was sensitive and poignant. Ball wisely eliminated both intermission and curtain calls, no doubt further to convey the intensity of his interesting interpretation. The uses of adversity may not be so sweet for theater companies, but in this case they did at least bring out the group's inventiveness. Dramatic lighting, gray flats, and brilliantly tawdry Goodwill Renaissance costumes all demonstrate the elasticity of dedicated theater people. The scientist who epitomizes the dehumanization of the modern world in his experiments on Woyzeck is done as a German burlesque comic, circa 1900, complete with fright wig and music-hall accent. This somewhat risky portrayal was probably meant to point to the general horror inherent in such experiments, and mirrors Woyzeck's own growing madness. In the end the interpretation of the scientist was an honorable failure, one worth attempting, and it did not really detract from the general effect of the production. The group as a whole shows a refreshingly unjaded dedication that one expects, but does not always encounter, in the small theater organizations.

Admission was $2.00, and a parking lot conveniently adjoins the theater.

Theatre of Involvement

331 Seventeenth Avenue Southeast, Minneapolis. 331-1891.

In our sweet youth, our church basement was known rather elegantly as an undercroft, and we attended Sunday School there. Having for many years now visited religious institutions for the purpose of admiring aspects of their architecture, we find it startling to contrast those youthful memories with what goes on in church basements today. An example is the Theatre of Involvement in the building of the United Ministries in Higher Education, which five Protestant denominations maintain near the Minneapolis campus of the University of Minnesota. In a long, low-ceilinged, unairconditioned cellar room we saw this company's production, directed by Joseph Rassulo, of Cryer and Ford's *The Last Sweet Days of Isaac*, starring John Martin and Susan Moos, accompanied (when dialogue gave way to music) by three singers and four instrumentalists. A young man and a young woman are trapped in an elevator in the "Elevator Play" portion of this pair of one-act plays. The power (read "modern society"?) has failed, and they are face to face with themselves, and with each other. As a kind of savior who is in his thirties and believes he is soon to die — this being the one suggestion of anything religious in the "Elevator Play" — the man seeks to keep the woman from drawing back from life by saying that the awareness of death shows us that life must be lived, must not be wasted. Death makes life possible. An old theme, with no particularly new development here — but it is all done with energy and occasional funny lines, and there is a nice irony at the end when he draws her out of herself only to find that she is now thinking of another man instead of yielding to his advances. Though the play was called by one critic a rock musical, only some of the music is rock (and this indeed is lively and, thank god, not overamplified); still other songs are reminiscent of the sentimental Broadway musicals of the 1940's.

The Last Sweet Days of Isaac was jointly produced by the Theatre of Involvement and the St. Paul Public Schools/Performing Arts Learning Center. The Theatre of Involvement itself is under the artistic direction of the Reverend William A. Livingston. Its productions have included such works as *The Tiger, The White Liars*, and *Once upon a Mattress*. Admission when we attended was by donation, and tickets can be reserved by telephone.

University of Minnesota Theater

University of Minnesota, Minneapolis. 373-2337.

The University of Minnesota's theater group regularly presents old and modern classics as well as some new plays each season. To have an idea of the heights to which it reaches, note that H. Wesley Balk's dramatization of *365 Days* (based on Ronald Glasser's book) was selected as the regional entry in 1972 for the National College Theater Festival in Washington, D.C., and dramatic critics were moved by its portrayal of how the Vietnam War ate viciously into a generation of young Americans. Tennessee Williams pronounced Debra Mooney's Blanche in *Streetcar Named Desire* one of the best he had ever seen. Other highlights have included Ibsen's *Doll's House* and Shakespeare's *Two Gentlemen of Verona*. Some seasons back we were lucky enough to see a superb *Antony and Cleopatra* and a magnificent production of Pirandello's *Six Characters in Search of an Author*. One cannot always expect such pinnacles, but this is meant to demonstrate that it is a theater well worth taking seriously. During the summer of 1972 a new play, N. Richard Nash's *Echoes*, proved that even less-than-great works receive serious, highly competent directing and acting. The concern with appearance and reality, and the conviction that the truly sane people are those who prefer to remain insane, is given a somewhat limp treatment, with more than its share of neo-Saroyan whimsy. The two lost people were quite well done by Elizabeth Rukavina and Gregg Almquist, though the playwright failed to make them very interesting characters. But a theater group should occasionally be judged by a mediocre play as well as the best plays, and director Stephen Kanee's wringing anything out of this one shows that it is a viable group. The University Theater's home in the new University performing arts building on the West Bank will be an improvement, but it has demonstrated its ingenuity by doing much with little in Scott Hall.

University Showboat

Minneapolis campus landing, University of Minnesota, on east bank of Mississippi River slightly south of Washington Avenue Bridge. 373-2337.

From June to early September — primarily at the University's landing, but also at landings elsewhere on the Mississippi River — the University Theater presents light to albino-light productions in its little gem of a theater on a genuine old riverboat. Year after year they play to packed houses (while some of the really serious groups in the Twin Cities feel lucky to scrape up an audience of thirty), so what follows does not necessarily represent the majority opinion.

At times productions on the Showboat have leaned toward camp, as in the case of *Billy the Kid* and *Forty-five Minutes from Broadway* in years past, but the 1972 offering of Oscar Hammerstein II and Jerome Kern's *Showboat* was not much of anything but sugar water, vintage 1939 (the kind that had turned sour by 1941). In a tiny theater, many of the actors shouted lines as if projecting from the stage of Northrop Auditorium. An antiquated view of racial relationships emerges despite whatever may have been done to make it more realistic. The gooey love story, stock characters, and unfunny humor make one wonder why something better couldn't have been found to spend time and money on. Fortunately, at other times the Showboat has used more promising material than this Hammerstein-Kern chestnut. Its second production in 1972 was Jean Giraudoux's *The Madwoman of Chaillot*. And the river is lovely on a soft summer evening, the boat charming, and its theater reminiscent of an elegant river-packet saloon with its face lifted, in green and gold.

For tickets and information, consult the University Theatre's ticket office in Scott Hall on the Minneapolis campus, whose telephone number is given above.

Dance

There is a rather wide spectrum of styles to be seen among dance companies in the Twin Cities, as will be evident in the descriptions here. In addition to the groups listed, the Northern Theatre Ballet, directed by Hi Summers, has grown out of the Minneapolis Ballet Company, and Ronald Holbrook's Feast of the Circle Dancers have drawn attention to vital Afro-American dance traditions. Also, during the 1971–1972 season the Walker Art Center sponsored a series of young choreographers' evenings, in which they had an opportunity to demonstrate their art.

Andahazy Ballet Borealis

1680 Grand Avenue, St. Paul. 698-8786.

The oldest classical dance company in the region, the Andahazy Ballet Borealis was founded in 1952 by Loran Andahazy and his wife, Anna Adrianova, in connection with their ballet school. Both directors have danced with the Russian Ballet in Europe and have worked with Michael Fokine, Leonid Massine, Pablo Picasso, and Igor Stravinsky. In a performance of *Les Sylphides* given at O'Shaughnessy Auditorium in a joint concert with the Apollo Club, the high polish and professionalism of the Andahazy Dance Company was evident under trying circumstances, for the recorded music failed for a considerable portion of the performance, yet perfect harmony was maintained, the dancers continuing with absolute poise. If the audience was momentarily startled, we soon forgot the mechanical failure in our fascination with these professionally trained and beautifully choreographed dancers. While *Les Sylphides* jars a bit today and the scenery is reminiscent of stale 1910 travel-ing troupes, this is a company maintaining high standards in a demanding, traditional art form.

Classical Ballet Academy of Minnesota

311 Ramsey Street, St. Paul. 222-4676.

The Minneapolis Tribune columnist Mike Steele has observed that dance is the fastest growing of the performing arts in the Upper Midwest, and one of the manifestations of this is the Classical Ballet Academy, founded by Jo Savino in 1971. A native St. Paulite, Savino has danced with the Ballet Russe de Monte Carlo and with companies in Germany, Switzerland, Belgium, Holland, France and Yugoslavia among others. Using classical ballet techniques he does, nevertheless, turn to modern themes. Rya Lee, formerly with the Chicago Opera Ballet Company, has recently joined the Classical Ballet Academy as principal dancer and teacher. The company presents performances in both cities; for information about them, contact the Academy.

Minnesota Dance Theater

Performances at various sites. 404 Thirteenth Avenue Southeast, Minneapolis. 331-5311.

Loyce Houlton has built up from her Minnesota School of Dance a bright, well-trained young troupe of dancers whose work falls somewhere between classical and modern dance. The group has more than once been invited to perform at the Jacob's Pillow Dance Festival in Lee, Massachusetts. Further proof of the professionalism of the Minnesota Dance Theater is Doris Herring's comment in *Dance Magazine*

(July 29, 1971) that the company "is rapidly realizing one's hope for America's decentralized dance companies — an identity with increasingly secure classical roots." The group performs with the Minnesota Symphony several times a year, doing an annual production of *The Nutcracker Suite* during the Christmas season. But the dancers should be seen on their less glamorous home territory, the Cedar Village Theater, 416 Cedar Avenue, Minneapolis. For in spite of poor sight lines, caused in part by the inadequate slope of the seating floor, the dancers give a polished performance with a wide range. In *Distant Figures* the suggestion of the unreality of the dream is somewhat too candy-boxish in its sweetness. But *Troth* is a beautifully staged depiction of the eternal sexual tug of war, ending in the inevitable killing. The pièce de résistance of this particular performance was *Mythical Hunters*, choreographed for the company when it travelled to Italy in 1971. The brilliant but spare use of props does not detract, and, as it should, enhances the effect of the dance; its culmination was in a huge net which trapped the hunted creature. While the dance is esthetically pleasing in itself, other levels of meaning are evoked, the hunting down and curbing of spontaneity in all creatures so that the harness of "civilization" brings to one dead level every spirit. The group shows what happens when hard work, talent, and the dedication of performers and director coalesce. Tickets were available at the door, priced moderately.

Nancy Hauser Dance Company

Guild of Performing Arts, 504 Cedar Avenue, Minneapolis. 333-8269.

If a near-capacity crowd for an opening night of the Nancy Hauser Dance Company was any indication, this area is now a hangout for culture vultures in the best sense of the

term. The highlight of the evening was Mrs. Hauser's *Beginnings*, a kind of dancer's digest of Evolution. A backdrop of projected slide images was very effectively coordinated with sound to enhance the movement of the dancers from creation, to insect, bird, animal, pre-man man and ritual, all showing what art can do that discursive prose misses. The mystery, the weirdness of the universe were conveyed in the opening projections of swirls, fires, rocks and the subsequent dramatic use of the projections on the dancers themselves intensified the eerieness. As a contrast to such an intense piece (which of course was wisely saved until last) Richard Haisma choreographed and danced the central role in *Mocking Song on the Spirit of Gravity*, a charmingly comic satire on man's pathetic dependence on the universe. The amusing-looking Haisma devised for himself a role in which he leaned, fell, etc. with fantastic control, all the while suggesting the pull of gravity. The Nancy Hauser Dance Company is very much in the tradition of modern dance and is one of the groups we strongly urge you to see.

Note: The Company uses the Cedar Village Theater at 416 Cedar Avenue, Minneapolis, for some productions, but it is advisable to telephone the Guild of Performing Arts for information on any particular performance.

Music

The state of the art is strong in the case of music. There is, at some seasons of the year, an embarrassment of riches. Our own selection includes a jazz establishment and a coffeehouse, but seeks primarily to suggest the variety of serious music available among permanently established groups.

Apollo Club of Minneapolis

3033 Excelsior Boulevard, Minneapolis. 922-7671.

This choral club is nearly eighty seasons old. It is an all-male group of some seventy voices (in the case of the concert we heard at the I. A. O'Shaughnessy Auditorium on the College of St. Catherine Campus in St. Paul), and it is competent in voice and energetically led by Raymond Cutting with accompaniment by Eileen Reagan and Lorraine King Wiklander on pianos. In appearance it could not be more staid and solid. A large number of the men are of middle age or more, and there is very little long hair (indeed, there is very little hair) in the ensemble. They were, in the performance we attended, white-tied, black-tailed, and white-carnationed, and the accompanists wore long white gowns. But one does not want to dwell too long on appearance. As to the music, the Club performs songs by everyone from Bach (J. S.) to Cohan (George M.), with Beethoven, Bruckner, Verdi, Wagner, Gounod, and others in between. The results were mixed, with such works as Bach's *Der Herr Segne Euch* and his *Sheep May Safely Graze* being quietly sonorous and nicely modulated. If you enjoy choral music, sample the Apollo Club's offerings.

Bach Society of Minnesota

One of the most invigorating aspects of the Twin Cities is the plethora of fine musical and theater groups for those of us who prefer to remain mere spectators, but also for the more energetic part-time participant. The Bach Society of Minnesota is undoubtedly one of the most accomplished and innovative of these organizations, drawing on the community at large for its membership, but including professional singers, church organists, choir directors, high school and college directors, and graduate students in music. One must audition for membership and fortunately some places become vacant each year, so that it is not a closed corporation. As a fitting personification of the group's vitality, Director David LaBerge manages successfully to combine twin careers as a member of the University of Minnesota's psychology department and director of the Bach Society. Patricia Porter and David Thomas are assistant directors. Since 1959 the Society has presented an annual Bach Festival in addition to making numerous appearances with local groups such as the Minnesota Symphrony, St. Paul Chamber Orchestra, and Center Opera Company. Within the Society, which consists of 220 members, is a Chamber Chorale of about 44 singers, which represented this country at the Manitoba Centennial in Winnipeg in 1970. The Bach Festival features one major work plus one other choral program in which cantatas, concerti, and suites are performed, in addition to an organ recital by Dr. Heinrich Fleischer, eminent Bach organist and scholar. The repertory is not limited to works by Bach, but includes Verdi's *Requiem*, Beethoven's *Ninth Symphony*, Haydn's *Creation*, (to name only a few compositions) as well as Bach's *Mass in B Minor, Magnificat, St. Matthew Passion, Christmas Oratorio*, and *St. John Passion*. For information on concerts and auditions, call 698-3646.

Center Opera Company of Minnesota

1503 Washington Avenue South, Minneapolis. 333-0509.

If you like opera, you will not want to depend alone on the Met's brief annual visit to Northrop Auditorium at the University of Minnesota and will want to see the professionally polished Center Opera Company. It says of itself that it is "the nation's only resident, professional and experimental lyric-theater ensemble," a statement, by the way, which is one of the many indexes of the degree to which the Twin Cities are committed to the arts. The Company is in residence for upwards of thirty weeks each year, and during that period presents existing operas and commissioned works such as *Postcard from Morocco* by Dominick Argento and John Donahue and the collage-opera *Faust Counter Faust*. Another example is *The Good Soldier Schweik* based on Jaroslav Hašek's novel about a subject of the dying Austro-Hungarian Empire in World War I who blandly faces the worst that bureaucracy can offer him. The music is by Robert Kurka, and the libretto in English by Lewis Allen. As is true of virtually all opera, the need to sing the story slows the pace of the theater that the performance in part consists of — but to its credit the Company was in very good voice, when we heard it, the accompaniment through a back-of-the-stage door of an orchestra under Philip Brunelle was highly competent, and the costumes (which were made in the Center Opera's own workshops) were positively dazzling in expressing the characters as symbols of the lowly citizen and of the official in society. General Manager of the Opera is John M. Ludwig, Brunelle is music director and administrator, H. Wesley Balk is stage director, and the company includes Vern Sutton (tenor) who portrayed Schweik, Barbara Brandt (soprano), and other professional singers. The range of the Company's offerings can be suggested not only by the works cited above, but also by the following: *Sir John in Love, The Rake's Progress, The Mother of Us All, Punch and Judy,* and *The Business of Good Government.* In the 1971—72 season the Center Opera played to 19,750 people, having toured Minnesota towns, Chicago, New York, Philadelphia, and Washington, D.C.

Concentus Musicus Renaissance
Vocal and Instrumental Ensemble

116 Warwick Avenue Southeast, Minneapolis 55414.

Such groups as the Concentus Musicus Renaissance Ensemble make the Twin Cities a truly civilized place in which to live. The Ensemble's aim, to make Renaissance music as alive as are the period's visual arts, is enhanced by colorful, evocative costumes. We were particularly fortunate to hear the group of eight instrumentalists at the Minneapolis Institute of Arts in the company of Rembrandt and Rubens. A variety of woodwinds ranging from curved (umbrella-handled) krumhorns to miniature flutes made us aware of the much greater range of sound than one finds in many compositions for a modern orchestra. Tambourines, the modern trombone's ancestor, the sackbut, a harpsichord, a most charming lute, all contribute to bring alive a nearly lost but worthy period of music. Who would expect to hear the rigal, a small handpumped organ, in duet with a tambourine? It was nearly as delightful as the limpid duet by the lute and cello. But this is one case where singling out individual performances is unfair because all players helped to recreate an atmosphere so redolent of the Renaissance that one sees bluff artisans, duennas and their charges, and a cardinal or two in the next piazza. The program included compositions, mostly quite short, from the courts of Ferdinand and Isabella and of their rivals in Italy, France, and England.

For information about membership in the Minnesota Friends of the Renaissance, write to the address above.

Extemporé Coffeehouse

325 Cedar Avenue, Minneapolis. 332-1023.

The Extemporé is all particular substance and very little polish. One searches for this coffeehouse in the University student's Latin Quarter flung out along several blocks of Cedar Avenue, and at last finds a modest exterior muttering its presence. The door gives onto a room where some sit playing chess, others talk quietly, and some eat the varied and inexpensive meals prepared there, which can include soup, macaroni, sandwiches, pudding, pastries, coffee (of course), teas, and juices.

A modest fee admits one to whatever musical entertainment is offered. But finding it is another matter. Finally, you locate a barnlike room virtually innocent of decoration, with paintflaked ceiling, no-nonsense wooden chairs, and a few soft chairs set (inexplicably) so high off the floor that the occupants' legs dangle. In one corner is a large, white refrigerator, whose after end faces the room's center. It is obviously unused. But the p.a. system is very much in order, with microphones set at both mouth level and guitarstring level, and from these we heard, first, folksinger David Hughes do songs, some or all of his own composition. Then appeared Jericho Harp, in fact two singers who accompany themselves on guitars and a harmonica: "It don't mean a thing to me. Why the hell pay for trouble when it's free?" Next a railroad song. Then a song about that devil, time.

The calendar offers other music — folk, jazz, blues — and a weekly discussion series on topics such as the Baha'i faith, abortion, the environment, scientology, and gay lib. On Saturday night (and presumably other evenings) blue jeans abound, onstage and off, but squarish guidebook writers of indeterminate middle age are accepted comfortably without stares. In fact, the atmosphere *is* congenial, that of the unselfconscious naturalness of a student coffeehouse.

Hall Brothers Emporium of Jazz

400 D Street, Mendota. 722-9404 for reservations, or 729-7179 for information; after 8 p.m. call 452-9922.

Across the Mendota Bridge, south of the Twin Cities, lies the town of Mendota, but it sleepeth not. It has long been the home of deep-grained New Orleans jazz, as practiced by the Hall Brothers Jazz Band, sometimes abetted by, or alternating from time to time with, visitors such as guitarist Eddie Condon and trumpeter Wild Bill Davidson or the Barry Marty International Ragtime Jazz Band from London.

The exterior of the Emporium, facing the Sibley Tea House on a side street in Mendota, is an unprepossessing hunk of white stucco. Inside: a plain paneled look, nothing fancy, with photographs and paintings of jazz musicians on the walls. Booths and tables are packed rather closely together, and there is a long bar along one wall. Pizza and fish and chips are available, and there are mixed drinks, beer (a bottle of Budweiser costs 50¢, which is not bad), and soft drinks. Jazz recordings are also sold.

A table or booth at a distance from the bandstand is recommended, for the music is amplified by a microphone. But *music* it is — plain, direct, honest New Orleans jazz, improvised in part, and in part arranged (for example, in some of the ensemble passages). The group consists of Charles De Vore on cornet, who also announces the numbers; Butch Thompson, clarinet; Russ Hall, trombone; Mike Polad, soprano saxophone and banjo (he also offered some ragtime piano music in mid-evening when we were there); Stan Hall, piano; Bill Evans, bass; and Don Berg, drums.

They are good, very good. They play well together, their solos are inventive.

The first set of the evening is apt to be a group of lesser-known but interesting pieces, such as *Working Man Blues*, Fats Waller's *Let's Break the Good News*, *Blue Bells Goodbye* (a march associated with the legendary Buddy Bolden), and *Chimes Blues*, which is based on a sacred work, *The Holy City*, and features the piano. Favorites are played in later sets — *Bill Bailey* is one — and the band will respond to a request like one for *The Panama Rag*. The names of the songs suggest the variety of music offered: blues, rags, marches, old popular songs susceptible of a jazz interpretation. And there are stomps and spirtuals. But the manner is that of New Orleans, that of the direct statement about life — sadness when you're sad, joy when you're happy, slow music and tears on the way to the funeral, liveliness breaking through on the way back. Life must go on.

As for dancing at the Emporium, forget it, unless you're willing to be more or less on display in a little alcove right next to the bandstand.

Admission on the evening we were there was a mere $1.50, but on some occasions the price is higher. Reservations are advisable at times, and in any event we suggest you telephone first for information about the schedule of performances.

Minneapolis Civic Orchestra

Charles Sigmund, interim assistant conductor; Barbara Wallace, manager; Shirley Thomson concertmistress. For a discussion of this full-complement orchestra see description of performance of Britten's *War Requiem* under University of Minnesota Chorus.

Minnesota Chamber Soloists

For information about concerts contact Carl Nashan, 922-8180.

The already musically pampered denizens of the Twin Cities were in July, 1970, presented with one more fine musical ensemble, the Minnesota Chamber Soloists, twelve members of the Minnesota Orchestra who formed this smaller group in order to perform music written for string ensembles. The performing of chamber music is the most demanding of all group playing since each member can be heard clearly. And the demands of musical democracy are carried out in the organization of the Minnesota Chamber Soloists, for there is no leader, each performer at times having the opportunity to play solo performances and with the leading parts regularly switched around. We can attest to their unusually high quality for a recording of the group has been much played and listened to in the Ervin home. The Corelli *Concerto Grosso in D-Major* (Opus 6, #4) is undoubtedly our favorite, but Hindemith's *Five Pieces for String Orchestra*, an aggregate of highly demanding compositions, Mozart's *Divertimento in D-Major*, k. 136, and the Vivaldi *Concerto in B-Minor for Four Violins* (Op. 3, #310) all attest to the high standards of The Chamber Soloists: They are currently in residence at the College of St. Catherine in St. Paul.

Minnesota Orchestra

Office: 110 Northrop Auditorium, University of Minnesota, Minneapolis. 373-2331.

Summing up the Minnesota Symphony a few years ago, a *Time* article was entitled "Big Five Plus One?" — thus indicating the very high quality of the Symphony. And in 1970 Donal Henahan, writing in the *New York Times*, observed that "It is today arguably among the nation's top six or seven orchestras in quality and probably the most important regional orchestra anywhere." But there is no need to become involved in the rating game, for the quality of the Minnesota Symphony has been recognized for many decades. Founded in 1903 as the Minneapolis Symphony, it has had a long and distinguished career. Such luminaries as Eugene Ormandy, Dmitri Mitropoulos, and Antal Dorati had already placed the Symphony among the nation's best when Stanislaw Skrowaczewski, a former conductor of the Warsaw Philharmonic, took over the leadership in 1960. Under Skrowaczewski the Orchestra has continued to grow both in size and in quality. The season has been expanded vertically and horizontally, for, in addition to a greater number of programs, during the regular season the performances are given first on Thursday evening in O'Shaughnessy Auditorium at the College of St. Catherine in St. Paul and on Friday at the more gargantuan Northrop Auditorium on the University of Minnesota's campus. Recognizing the importance of exposing audiences to new music if they are ever to enjoy it, and resisting the temptation to fall back on old chestnuts as the only fare, Skrowaczewski, a composer of avant-garde music himself, has given more weight to modern music than did his predecessors. That the maestro has no timidity in such matters was evident in one bizarre concert in which the Swingle Singers were on hand to perform Berio's *Sinfonia*. Ward Swingle located his singers in Parisian bistros and developed them into a unit which emitted sounds strangely inhuman. But our more conservative tastes were amply compensated by a rare performance of Berlioz's *Harold in Italy* featuring the orchestra's principal violist, Lawrence Wheeler. The following will give an idea of the musical smorgasbord from which you can choose in a typical season: Stravinsky's *Suite from the Ballet "Pulcinella,"* Debussy's *La Mer*, Brahms' *Piano*

129

Concerto #2; Beethoven's *Overture to Coriolanus*, Dvořák's *Cello Concerto* (played by Janos Starker), Stravinsky's *Firebird Suite*, Lutosloswski's *Cello Concerto* and Haydn's *Concerto for Cello in C Major* (both played by Mstislav Rostropovich), Shostakovich's *Symphony #8*; Haydn's *Symphony #67*, Hindemith's *Violin Concerto*, Schumann's *Symphony #4*. A performance of Beethoven's *Ninth Symphony* with the Bach Society Chorus was presented in June after the regular season.

At least one guest conductor is featured every season. The lighter Sunday Afternoon Concerts balance the diet of the more ambitious Thursday and Friday offerings, and for many years the orchestra has offered afternoon concerts to school children in which something of the structure and theme of the music is explained after the performance. An abbreviated summer season leans to popular items, but in recent years more serious concerts have been working their way onto the summer agenda. The orchestra has also been taking music to the people in a variety of ways, with free park concerts and other variations on this happy theme.

St. Paul Chamber Orchestra

30 East Tenth Street, St. Paul. 225-6571.

Founded in 1959, the St. Paul Chamber Orchestra is the only resident professional chamber orchestra in the United States, and now has twenty-two full-time musicians. For a number of years the orchestra has attracted world-famous soloists such as harpsichordist Ralph Kirkpatrick, cellist Janos Starker, and flutist Jean Pierre Rampal, but more important than the frosting of the big-name soloists is the fact that the orchestra itself has maintained high standards of performance and has set a fine example of taking music to the people. Depending upon the environment, the orchestra can be broken up into small ensembles of string quartets, a woodwind quartet, and a baroque ensemble playing for schools, hospitals, libraries, community centers,and residences for senior citizens. One winter a series of free Sunday afternoon concerts were given at the Minneapolis Institute of Arts. And the orchestra's recently inaugurated summer sandwich serenade concerts enliven the lunch hour of downtown St. Paulites who walk to Rice Park or the Arts and Science Center. We have revelled in the superabundance of Mozart, Bach, Haydn, Beethoven, and Handel, but the group also ventures into more modern music. Dennis Russell Davies was appointed to direct the orchestra beginning with the 1972–73 season.

St. Paul Opera Association

143 West Fourth Street, St. Paul. 227-3046.

That the Cities have two operatic organizations of the caliber of the Center Opera Company and the St. Paul Opera Association, which is now in its fortieth year, attests to the breadth of musical interest and support in the community at large. The St. Paul Opera has in recent years instituted a regular summer repertory program, one of whose productions we attended. While the Center Opera tends to attract the pants suits and vinyl shoes, the St. Paul Opera audience is graced by long-skirted ladies squired by gentlemen in that nearly forgotten sartorial item, the dinner jacket. The audience reflects the St. Paul Opera's tendency to take on less adventurous productions than does its opposite number. *Madam Butterfly*, while not calculated to thrill those seeking innovation, was a beautiful and professionally polished production which did justice to Puccini's music. Sets and costumes designed by Ming Cho Lee were exquisite, so that the evening was as much a feast for the eye as for the ear. Nancy Shade, Vahan Khanzadian, and Vern Shinal in the roles of Butterfly, Pinkerton, and Sharpless, respectively, and all singers with national reputations, demonstrated their professionalism in their performances. The orchestra was conducted by Edwin MacArthur, whose familiarity with the score was evident in his past record; he once conducted 75 performances of *Butterfly* in 77 days. Two other ingredients absolutely necessary for successful music and theater of any kind, good acoustics and a highly receptive and sympathetic audience, helped to round out a successful evening. The St. Paul Opera has given the world premiere of Carl Neilsson's *Maskarade*. It has also premiered an operatic version of Tennessee Williams' *Summer and Smoke*, which received high acclaim from critics in other cities. Prices of tickets range from $3.50 to $8.50.

Schubert Club

St. Paul Arts and Science Center, 30 East Tenth Street, St. Paul. 222-6122.

The most venerable of Twin Cities musical organizations, the Schubert Club celebrated its ninetieth season in 1972. Its quiet contribution to the enrichment of musical life in the area is one of its most noteworthy features, for while it is probably best known for the international artists whose local appearances it sponsors, other activities provide opportunities for local artists to perform for the public in unpretentious surroundings. The highly polished Schubert Boys Club choir was chosen to perform with the Minneapolis Civic Orchestra and University of Minnesota chorus when Kurt Adler conducted all three groups in Benjamin Britten's *War Requiem* in 1972. An Active Artists Section — made up of professional and amateur musicians — does much to take music into the schools, performing and explaining music to children, and professional musicians present a Daytime Concert Series in the morning. The Schubert's student section provides scholarships for young musicians as well as sponsoring Sunday concerts in which student musicians perform. In addition to its musical activities the Schubert Club has provided one of the more interesting local film series, reviving a worthy group of French films and offering a Russian series. A telephone call will place you on its mailing list.

University of Minnesota Chorus

Directed by Charles Schwartz. On June 1, 1972, in a free concert in the University's Northrop Auditorium, the University Chorus, the Schubert Club Boys' Choir, and the Minneapolis Civic Orchestra, with three vocal soloists, performed Benjamin Britten's *War Requiem* under the baton of Kurt Adler, conductor and chorus master at the Metropolitan Opera and an authority on the art (he is the author of *The Art of Accompanying and Coaching* and *Phonetics and Diction in Singing*). The performance was a demanding one, for the word concert in the sense of complex musical consonance must apply to a rendition of the *Requiem*. And concert it was, which is a testimony not only to Adler but also to the abilities of the University Chorus, the Schubert Club Boys' Choir, and the Minneapolis Civic Orchestra.

Britten completed the *Requiem* in 1961 for the rededication of Coventry Cathedral, which had been bombed in World War II. The *Requiem* is a setting of the Latin Mass for the Dead and poems of Wilfred Owen, one of the generation of English poets of the First World War, who returned to the front after being hospitalized for a wound and was killed in action, aged twenty-five, one week before the armistice. "All a poet can do is warn," he wrote. The ambitious scale of the work, the abilities of the performers, and the theme of man's grief for man in time of war must have had much appeal, for a large audience was in attendance, while not every free event has such attractiveness.

Historic Sites

This listing of historic sites includes no private houses, with the exception of the F. Scott Fitzgerald home, which has been designated a National Historic Landmark. Certain buildings which seemed most appropriately placed in the section entitled Points of Architectural and Artistic Interest — such as the two Pillsbury homes in Minneapolis, the Cathedral of St. Paul, and the Minnesota State Capitol Building — are of historical importance as well.

Burbank-Livingston-Griggs Mansion
432 Summit Avenue, St. Paul. 227-1343.

When Scott Fitzgerald remarked that "the very rich are different from you and me," he might well have had in mind the Burbank-Livingston-Griggs House, an American Civil War–Italianate–Victorian mansion built of Mendota limestone. The American desire to recreate Europe in middle America, usually expressed in eclectic collecting, is here carried to an extreme which only the very *very* rich could afford, for with the exception of the hallway and the Stone Room, each room was dismantled and brought from French and Italian eighteenth- and early nineteenth-century homes. Although the mansion had been built in the 1860's by riverboat operator James Burbank, its Europeanization took place in the 1930's under the aegis of Mary Livingston Griggs, a descendant. Judging from what remains of the original Victorian décor — the carved oak hallway in the worst of ornate American tastelessness — Mrs. Griggs did well to turn to eighteenth- and early nineteenth-century Europe. Eclecticism prevails still, for the eighteenth-century Venetian dining room, with its green panelled walls and its marble floors, is furnished with English Sheraton furniture. The late eighteenth-century mirror room (supposedly inspired by the Hall of Mirrors at Versailles) undoubtedly had as its immediate predecessor such Parisian townhouses as the Hôtel de Soubise. From the delicate rococo panelling and Louis XV and XVI furniture one can gain an excellent notion of the apogee of good taste which preceded Victorian overstatement. The mirrors have gone awry, but again with a little stretch of the imagination one can see in the alternation of mirrors and windows the striving for light and delicacy brought to perfection during the twilight of the ancien régime. Unquestionably the loveliest acquisition is a Louis XV sitting room, with a teardrop chandelier, fine rococo carving, and furniture perfectly proportioned to its intimate size. Of the mansion's many eyeopeners the prize must go to the red marble bathtub carved from a single block of Carrara marble, forty inches deep, and about thirty-six inches in length! Nor for small children or anyone at the backache stage! A microcosmic expression of what appears to be the self-indulgence of the very rich is a beautifully appointed doll house, where even the table service is of sterling silver. In her Europeanization of Summit Avenue, Mrs. Griggs did not entirely resist one American extravagance, for the art-deco recreation room, with its marble floors, silver-tinted ceilings, and poshy bathrooms, is

straight out of a Jean Harlow film. Burbank chose a dramatic site for his mansion, overlooking the river, but now unfortunately commanding a mostly industrial view of St. Paul. While the B-L-G is not a complete success aesthetically, it is well worth a visit for its best features and, in general, as a late manifestation of the desire to bring Paris to Pig's Eye!

An extremely knowledgeable and courteous guide explains the fine points of the mansion, which is now owned by the Minnesota Historical Society, with the Junior League of St. Paul assisting in its management. Note that the entrance is at a side door, and watch for the flight of steps as you open the door.

Falls of St. Anthony, Pillsbury "A" Mill, and Stone Arch Bridge

Visible from observation deck of upper lock, 1 Portland Avenue South, Minneapolis.

The falls, caused by a drop of seventy-five feet in the Mississippi, were discovered and named by Father Louis Hennepin in 1680 and became the kernel of Minneapolis history, for they supplied the power for the city's industrial bloodstream, sawmilling and flour milling. They were the site of a grist mill and sawmill from the early 1820's and in 1882 powered the first hydroelectric central station in the United States.

Across the river from the observation deck is the Pillsbury "A" Mill. Designed by L. S. Buffington and from 1881 to 1930 one of the largest flour mills in the world, it is not unlike a Florentine palazzo with its rock-faced limestone and a principal façade of subtly arranged arched window groups. Both historically and architecturally it is an important monument of Minneapolis history.

Burbank-Livingston-Griggs Mansion

Not far from the falls and as if to challenge nature, a magnificent stone bridge spans the river in a series of catenary arches and resembles a Roman bridge, demonstrating that man can actually enhance the beauty of nature. Designed by Colonel Charles Smith and built by James J. Hill as a railroad bridge to link the wheatfields of the Northwest with the flour mills, it was dubbed ''Jim Hill's folly'' when plans were announced for its construction in 1881, but was much praised upon its completion in 1883 and is now considered one of the finest stone bridges in the nation.

Faribault House

Mendota. Call Sibley House (452-1596) for information.

Though Jean Baptiste Faribualt, whose home this was, never achieved the eminence of his Mendota neighbor Henry Hastings Sibley, he was a knowledgeable and a picturesque French-Canadian trader and, as the dimensions of his house attest, a man of some means. After association with the Northwest Fur Company and management of several of its posts, he became an independent trader at Prairie du Chien, moving upriver to Pike Island (in the Mississippi River near Fort Snelling), from which floods drove him. In 1826 he established himself at Mendota, though he usually wintered at Little Rapids, thirty-five miles from Mendota. In 1836 Faribault built the present house, now open to the public under the aegis of the Minnesota DAR, of yellow limestone quarried in the area. Its simple exterior elegance allows it to join the Sibley House as an interesting affront to the more ornate dwellings so typical of the affluent later in the nineteenth century. Its restoration was begun by the Highway Department as a Public Works Administration project in 1935 — it is remarkable to think of highway people sometimes preserving houses, instead of displacing them or drowning them in traffic noise — and subsequently the house was turned over to the DAR.

F. Scott Fitzgerald Home

599 Summit Avenue, St. Paul.

The house in which in 1918 F. Scott Fitzgerald wrote *This Side of Paradise*, his first important book, has been designated a National Historic Landmark. It is part of a series of eight attached dwellings, an 1889 riot of octagonal witch's-cap turrets, bay windows, gables, and recessed doorways. It is privately owned and not open to the public, but drive by and down the length of Summit Avenue in order to evoke a feeling of the long-forgotten world of nineteenth-century elegance and particularly to conjure up the world that played so large a part in creating Amory Blaine, Jay Gatsby, and Dick Diver.

Fort Snelling

Restoration and Historic Area, just south of Twin Cities. 726-1171.

The restoration of Fort Snelling allows one to gain a feeling for life in preterriotrial Minnesota. Fort St. Anthony (later re-named for its builder and first commander, Colonel Josiah Snelling) was the northwestern link in the chain of forts built to keep peace with the Indians, to drive out foreign trade, and to serve as the local fur trade depot. It is located above the junction of the Minnesota and Mississippi Rivers and the ideal time for a visit is late spring, summer, or early autumn, when the beauty of the river valleys serves as a foil for the harsh, rugged outlines of the unadorned limestone buildings, fitting symbols of life in an outpost built to police 90,000 square miles. Guards dressed in white

fatigues of the Fifth Regiment in the 1820's willingly explain the various buildings and their uses, while young ladies in appropriate dress mind the store and generally recreate a pioneer woman's life. The sutler's store is stocked with wares one would have found here in the 1820's — hand-dipped candles (forty dips to a candle!), quill pens, slates, cast iron pots, clay pipes, barrels, and a few pretty glass bottles and pewter dishes to relieve the tedium of life on the fort. For a more harshly realistic reminder of life on an outpost, sit for awhile on the backless benches in the starkly whitewashed school/chapel. Or step into the guardhouse to conjure up a winter's residence in this stone building, dining on bread and water, a fairly frequent occurrence for enlisted men whose "ranks were filled with the ne'er do well, the shiftless and the troublesome" . . . where "drunkness and desertion were the common offenses; boredom and lethargy the common mood." The powder magazine's pegged floors are a testament to the dangers of life at the fort, for a spark from a solider's hob-nailed boot might have proved fatal.

The recreated fort is undoubtedly one of the most interesting historic landmarks in the area and (with the Gibbs Farm Museum) the most enjoyable for children, who delight in running from building to building, marching with the drummer, imagining themselves manning the cannon (which is fired at approximately 2:00 p.m. after much rehearsal time), and simulating sentry duty from an elevated platform on the round tower.

Gibbs Farm Museum

2097 West Larpenteur Avenue, St. Paul. 646-0624.

The Gibbs Farm Museum, at West Larpenteur and Cleveland Avenues, provides the best opportunity for Twin

Citians to step back into the life of a prosperous but hard-working pioneer family of the mid-nineteenth century. Owned and operated by the Ramsey County Historical Society, the museum actually consists of four buildings: the farmhouse, a one-room schoolhouse, and two barns. The spacious grounds with their comfortable old trees convey a different world from that of our revved-up era. The farmhouse home of Heman and Jane DeBow Gibbs was built on this site between 1854 and 1870, having grown from a one-room log cabin to a somewhat larger home. Here you can see a demonstration of the carding and spinning of wool, candle dipping, and other pioneer craft; each Sunday a particular craft receives special attention, but on other days one might see some of them. The house is not furnished entirely with the Gibbs family possessions, but gives an idea of life in a working family of the period. A spool bed made by Mr. Gibbs with spools high enough to hold a canopy is particularly noteworthy. Another bedroom holds a rack for quilting so that one can imagine the ladies busy at their "active leisure." While children are apt to enjoy the other buildings and the swings on the grounds more than the farmhouse, the house actually has something for everyone, including a dollhouse of somewhat greater elegance than the Gibbs home itself, arrowheads, a grandfather clock, and cradles.

The Old Stoen School, a one-room schoolhouse built in Chippewa County in 1878 and subsequently brought to the Gibbs Farm, is a far cry from today's "open school." With its stationary desks, dunce's cap, and hard slates all pointing toward teacher, very much in command in front — there was no democracy here. A very nice gentleman explains (to tour groups of children) a typical day in the life of a pioneer schoolchild. Each summer children from first through sixth grade may experience this by attending school for one day in groups of twenty.

The red barn (built in 1958 to house farm implements)

gives an excellent idea of the tools — such as cooper's tools, a variety of animal traps, hog-butchering knives, hewing and splitting tools, cider press, fishing and trapping equipment — needed to survive in rural America. The Studebaker buggy and the pony cart are more believably farm accouterments than the Vis-à-Vis and Victoria (owned by James J. Hill) housed in the white barn. But most significant for an idea of Minnesota necessities are the three sleighs, a double cutter, a Canadian cutter, and a Cabriolet sleigh. And, of course, there are a few animals around, a couple of largish sheep and a lamb, chickens, kittens, and bunnies (the last for sale at $2.00).

Ard Godfrey Cottage

Chute Square, Central and University Avenues Southeast, Minneapolis.

Built in 1849 by Ard Godfrey, a millwright who came to Minnesota to construct the first commercial sawmill, this is probably the oldest dwelling in that part of Minneapolis which was once St. Anthony. In this little house Harriet Godfrey was the first white child to be born in what is now Minneapolis, and here the Godfrey family entertained many early visitors to the area. The house is included in the National Historic Buildings Survey, but unfortunately is boarded up, with the result that many of its architecturally significant "classical revival" elements are obscured. It is not open to the public.

James J. Hill Residence

240 Summit Avenue, St. Paul.

The former residence of James J. Hill is a home befitting an era when it was still possible to build empires. Completed in 1891, it is constructed of red sandstone and, with its arched porte-cochere, many dormers, and tall chimneys, bespeaks the grandeur of a bygone era. Of it H. F. Koeper says in his *Historic St. Paul Buildings* that "the design is a picturesque assembly of parts and is believed by many to be the most successful, elaborate and largest Richardsonian residence built in Minnesota up to 1892." It is not open to the public.

Indian Mounds Park

Earl Street and Mounds Boulevard, St. Paul.

The plowing under of a large part of the original 10,000 Indian burial mounds by early Minnesota settlers has fortunately spared a group in the Indian Mounds Park in St. Paul. To the casual eye these are grass-covered hillocks of a strange but not too dramatically remarkable shape. But they are, as careful scientific excavations in other areas have shown, the repositories of dead Indians and their possessions. In them pottery, arrowheads, necklaces, and copper pieces have been found and much has been learned of Indian life from these excavations. They were built during the Woodland era, from 1,000 B.C. to the coming of the white man in the seventeenth and eighteenth centuries. In addition to giving the visitor a feeling for Minnesota prehistory, a trip to Mounds Park will provide him with a panoramic summary of the white man's potential burial sites. At a particularly attractive stretch of the river far below barges are drawn up near grain storage bins, across the river a municipal airport is alive with what appear to be toy airplanes to our Brobdingagian eyes grown accustomed to 747s, and highways and railroads abound. But the panorama embraces that delightful juxtaposition of pastoral and urban which typifies the Twin Cities, with a luxuriant growth of wild flowers and trees attracting song-birds. From our own experience the view suits the whole family — ma and pa can indulge their Wordsworthianism while the younger members will undoubtedly be more turned on by the questionable fruits of civilization.

Mattocks School

On the grounds of Highland Park Senior High School, 1015 Snelling Avenue South, St. Paul 690-1545.

This one-room schoolhouse, constructed of twenty-inch-thick native limestone blocks, opened in 1871 to serve Reserve Township, which was annexed by the city in 1887. Originally called Webster Number 9, it was in 1887 renamed for the Reverend John Mattocks, a prominent Presbyterian clergyman connected with the St. Paul schools. It was used as a classroom until 1929, from 1931 to 1961 served as an American Legion Post, and is once more functioning as a classroom on the grounds of the Highland Park Senior High School, to which it was moved within recent years. It was furnished to serve thirty children and retains many of its original features intact. Call Highland Park Senior High for information about the possibility of seeing this building, which has been included in the Historic American Buildings Survey.

Minnehaha Depot

Minnehaha Park, Minnehaha Avenue near East Forty-ninth Street, Minneapolis. 726-1171.

The Minnesota Historical Society administers this piece of nostalgia for a simpler era, a time when railroads actually offered the prolific passenger service that (in metropolitan areas at least) we ruefully find we may need again, now that we are being crushed by the intolerabilities of the once-proud automobile. The Minnehaha Depot is a small but charming gingerbread building, erected in 1875 to succeed a still smaller station, and serving such runs as that to and from Austin, Minnesota, and the summer excursions between downtown Minneapolis and the park and Longfellow Gardens Zoo. The trip was scheduled for sixteen minutes' duration in each direction, a figure that stands comparison with those by other modes today. The depot building and canopied platforms are the interesting elements here, with their Carpenter-Gothic or Steamboat-Gothic ornateness. As Donald Torbert points out in his book on *Significant Architecture in the History of Minneapolis*, such structures "exploited in greater or lesser degree the design potentials of the jig-saw and 'dimension' lumber." One thinks of them as fondly as one thinks of the gazebos, equally ornate, which once sheltered the thoughtful, the bored, or the lovestruck on long summer afternoons on the lawns of upper-class homes. Next to the depot is a railroad car, adding to the atmosphere. The work of restoration is that of the Minnesota Transportation Museum. Something of the car and the building may be seen easily by passersby at any hour or season, but you may wish to telephone to learn when you may enter them. Admission is free.

Muskego Church

On the campus of Luther Theological Seminary, Como Avenue and Luther Place, St. Paul.

This log meeting house, the first Norwegian Lutheran church in the United States, was built in 1843–44 by Norwegian immigrants at Muskego, Wisconsin. Used as a church for a number of years, it then became a barn, and was subsequently purchased by the United Lutheran Church of America and moved to St. Paul in 1904. Of the interior H. F. Koeper, in his *Historic St. Paul Buildings*, says "The inside walls are formed by massive red oak logs fitted tightly together and planed flat. They, like the pews, altar, pulpit, railings, and black walnut pillars supporting a U-shaped gallery, have never been painted and bear the marks of the adze and plane used in their construction. Simple furnishings, including a pump organ and wood-burning stove, complete the restoration." This church, included in the Historic American Buildings Survey, is open to the public upon request at the Seminary.

Alexander Ramsey House

265 South Exchange Street, St. Paul. 222-5717.

In 1849 Alexander Ramsey of Pennsylvania was offered the governorship of Minnesota Territory, and Mrs. Ramsey exclaimed, "Minnesota! Where upon earth is it? In Denmark?" Theodore Blegen, who records this in his book *Minnesota: A History of the State*, writes there of Ramsey: "A biographer of the governor, reviewing his early career, describes him as 'social, cool, cautious, and given to practical business.' These qualities, plus a maturing political sagacity, a readiness to accept responsibility, an intelligence that appraised the potentialities of the frontier community, a gift for incisive phrase, and a generous span of cultural interests that left imprints on Minnesota institutions and life, marked the man in a long and distinguished career embracing the governorship of both territory and state and service as a United States senator for a dozen years and as secretary of war (1879–81)." The Ramsey House reflects some of these attributes: It is the home of people who were culturally interested and aware. Some of the contents — for example, Dresden chairs — came from Europe; many

others were made in New York and shipped in. (A mounted animal head is presumably indigenous.) It is a social but cautious house. The principal room is the ballroom or large parlor, complete with Steinway; the room was closed sometimes in cold weather and the piano moved across the hall. In the hall itself there is a salver on a table for callers' cards. Also on the first floor are a small parlor, a sedate dining room, and the kitchen. Upstairs are bedrooms and Ramsey's study.

The interior is late-Victorian-overdone in appearance. Sixteen rooms, mostly overdecorated and heavy, patterned drapes clashing with patterned wallpaper, everything stuffed with furniture. A number of Oriental motifs are seen — here a screen, there an *objet*. The kitchen is sensible enough, with its wood stove, icebox, gingersnaps for visitors. And of course some of the elements in other rooms are individually attractive, for instance the acid-etched frosted glass toward the front of the first floor. It is just that there are too many elements, and they jostle each other.

But, asthetics aside, the house is historically interesting, for here a family of position and means built and lived and preserved its mode of life until 1964, when the home was willed to the Minnesota Historical Society by the Ramsey granddaughters.

And outdoors, aesthetics and history blend satisfactorily. A cast-iron fence is elegantly simple, and the construction of the house, in the French Renaissance style and of native limestone, with a mansard roof, is not altogether displeasing. A reasonably spacious lawn has plantings, including a lovely locust tree, and leads one to a carriage house, which also serves as a visitors' center, having been rebuilt in 1970 from its 1883 construction.

Admission, $1.00 for adults; no charge for children under 16 accompanied by an adult. School tours by reservation, 25¢ each pupil and teacher. Other groups by reservation.

Alexander Ramsey House

Sibley House

Mendota. 452-1596.

The waters of the Minnesota (formerly St. Peter's) and Mississippi rivers meet near here, below the bluffs, and this confluence helped make Mendota a site for an American Fur Company trading post. Henry Hastings Sibley was assigned by the company to the area, with Mendota as headquarters, and in 1834, a decisive young man of only twenty-three, he came to Minnesota. On his arrival, he "viewed the stone walls and towers of Fort Snelling," writes Theodore Blegen in his book *Minnesota: A History of the State*, "and came to the tiny village of Mendota with its crude log huts, in one of which . . . he lived for some time. Thus began the Minnesota career of a man destined to supervise an empire of furs, help to create Minnesota Territory and fashion Minnesota's constitution, serve as the first governor of the North Star state, command an army in an Indian war, and win renown as citizen and recorder of early Minnesota."

Mendota basked in the protection of nearby Fort Snelling. In 1835 Sibley built there one of the first private dwellings in the old Northwest, and it has esthetic as well as historical qualities, for its lines are ample and well-proportioned, and the stone is handsome. Inside there is less to be said esthetically, but the rooms and their furnishings, which are of the period of the 1850's and 1860's, are of historical interest. One also likes the fact that, as Blegen writes, this home "was a friendly spot where both whites and Indians found genial sanctuary."

When Sibley moved to St. Paul in 1862 he sold his home to St. Peter's Parish, and its career as a convent began. Later it was an art school, and — commerce revived! — a warehouse. Archbishop Ireland presented it to the Minnesota Daughters of the American Revolution, and under their guidance it was restored to its earlier appearance and opened to the public as a museum, which it remains today. Admission: adults, $1.00; children, 6 to 11, 25¢, and 12 to 18, 50¢; supervised groups of children admitted without charge, on advance reservation. Open in the summer and part of the spring and fall. Telephone regarding days and hours.

John M. Stevens House

Minnehaha State Park, Minneapolis.

In this house, built by Canadian John Stevens in 1850, the name "Minneapolis" was selected in 1852. Stevens was the first permanent settler on the west bank of the Mississippi, having been granted the right to build there in order to maintain a ferry for the crossing of troops from Fort Snelling. The house was originally on the riverbank near the present Great Northern Station, and was moved to its present site in 1896, with school children helping horses to pull the house. It is not open to the public.

"William Crooks" Engine

Lobby of St. Paul Union Depot, 214 East Fourth Street, St. Paul.

The first iron horse in Minnesota, this twenty-five-ton engine began regular service on July 2, 1862 on the ten-mile line from St. Paul to St. Anthony. Named for the chief engineer of the St. Paul and Pacific Railway, it burned wood in its early years; if the supply of wood gave out between woodpiles, nearby fences were used for fuel. While it could reach a speed of sixty miles an hour, it usually maintained a pleasant fifteen to twenty-five. The engine was retired in 1900, although it was kept in running condition until 1954.

Points of Artistic and Architectural Interest

Our selection of points of architectural interest includes buildings which are of particular note to us, esthetically or because of their significance in the history of construction in the area. For authoritative accounts of important buildings, we refer the reader to such works as *Significant Architecture in the History of Minneapolis* by Donald R. Torbert, with photographs by Eric Sutherland, and *Historic St. Paul Buildings* by H. F. Koeper, with photographs by Eugene Becker. Private homes have been deliberately omitted in this section, as some owners have had more than their share of tourists.

Butler Brothers Building

First Avenue North at Sixth Street, Minneapolis.

Not all of our buildings of architectural interest are to be found in the pristine glory of the Yamasaki building. Take a walk over to an unprepossessing corner of First Avenue North and Sixth Street to gain an idea of early twentieth-century use of Renaissance architecture for a warehouse. To anyone longing for a return to the Italian hill towns it will come as a pleasant shock to find this massive, fortresslike building with its San Gimignano towers, its Renaissance sense of perfect pitch in the use of recessed spandrels and pointed and segmental arch forms. The restraint in decoration is particularly noteworthy for its period. Designed by Harry Jones and built between 1906 and 1908, this is a building much admired by art historians and has been included by Donald Torbert in a group of local buildings which should be saved as part of our heritage. (See his *Significant Architecture in the history of Minneapolis*, with photographs by Eric Sutherland.)

Cathedral of St. Paul

Summit and Dayton Avenues, St. Paul. 225-6563.

Though they now have rivals in the office buildings and hotels of downtown St. Paul, the Cathedral and State Capitol still dominate the cityscape. Each is superbly situated on an eminence and so is visible from many directions and distances. The Cathedral, designed by the French-born architect Emmanuel L. Masqueray and built between 1906 and 1915, has as its most imposing feature its dome, and this proves to be so whether one is inside or out. The neo-baroque interior is lavishly decorated with colored marbles and stone carvings, and is fittingly topped with a dome which has a diameter of ninety-six feet. Other features include three interesting rose windows, and a baldaquin which is big and no better-looking than dozens of others, including that by the otherwise immortal Giovanni Lorenzo Bernini in St. Peter's in Rome. The Cathedral of St. Paul, then, is imposing for its site, its size, and on the whole a certain stateliness. Though an admirer of ecclesiastical architecture would surely not start a grand tour at the Cathedral, it merits visiting.

Christ Church Lutheran

3244 Thirty-fourth Avenue South, Minneapolis. 721-6611.

Religion as harmony, as reconciliation, is the theme one feels in the beautiful architectural statement made by this

moderately proportioned church. The congregation engaged
Eliel Saarinen, the Finnish architect, to design the building,
and he was assisted in this by his son, the celebrated Eero
Saarinen. Here in their work is no trumpet of the lord;
rather, one sees a church building and adjoining bell tower
standing quietly and serenely, not yielding their architectural
pleasures except as one looks closely and contemplates the
details and the way they work together. The stone façade
in beige is unadorned except for four small relief scuptures
showing groups of figures in a compellingly primitive
manner. In subtle contrast to the beige of the stone, there
is the beige brick of much of the rest of the handsome
church building and campanile — brick laid lengthwise
except that every seven courses or so the narrow ends are
seen in alternation with the lengthwise bricks. And the beige
is here and there punctuated by red- and wine-colored brick.
The campanile is accented at its top by a cross, and on
the south wall of the church there are three more crosses
in relief. All is successfully understated. The interior of
the church also makes use of beige, and bricks are again
employed to suggest quiet strength with patterns of contrasts
provided by bricks turned vertically in contrast to the hori-
zontal ones. The pews are light in color and not so warm
in feeling as the brick. This subtly beautiful edifice was
completed in 1949, and across a small courtyard from the
church and bell tower is a separately built annex dating
from 1962, also in beige.

Federal Courts Building

West Fifth Street at Market Street, St. Paul.

While late nineteenth- and early twentieth-century en-
thusiasm for neo-gothic structures resulted in some of the
Twin Cities' most tasteless buildings, the north side of Rice

154

Park in St. Paul is graced by a lovable old French Chateau — our own Chateau de Chenonceaux. Formerly the Federal Courts Building and recently acquired by St. Paul as a center for the arts, it was designed by James Knox Taylor and officially opened in 1902. It is a realization of picture-bookish conical turrets, gables, and magnificent towers, with steeply pitched roofs adding to the feeling of majesty thought necessary for a federal building of its day.

First Christian Church
2201 First Avenue South, Minneapolis.

This building designed by Thorshov and Cerny and built in 1954 has a strangely fortresslike appearance with a tall narrow façade pierced by small roundels of multicolored glass. A large free standing cross and a bell tower add to the effect of attenuation, of striving toward heaven. The interior is dark, but dramatically highlighted by brilliant colors of the roundels in the eastern end. The effect of the whole is that of the intensity of the tall, narrow French gothic churches and cathedrals. This is reflected further in the long, narrow arrangements of lights. The interior makes much use of decorating with building materials and has a fine, richly hued wooden ceiling, a subtly arranged brick altar wall, a huge but simple metal cross, and an altar looking for all the world like an expensive office desk, punctuated with a beautiful arrangement of flowers which provide the only color at this end of the church.

Fountain by Pietro Tacca
Coffman Memorial Union Courtyard, University of Minnesota, Minneapolis.

Few, probably, of the University's students and faculty

realize that in the courtyard of Coffman Memorial Union stands a delightful bronze fountain designed and executed in Florence in 1620 by Pietro Tacca, a pupil of the renowned Gianbologna. James Ford Bell brought the fountain to this country in 1920 and it was presented to the University by the Bell family in 1961. Part of a trio (the other two can be found in the Piazza della Santissima Annunziata in Florence), this exquisite work should remind us that art need not be serious and that it can serve a useful purpose. Two gamin-like sea monsters riding dolphins emit jets of water which cross those of the dolphins, water and sculpture creating together an air of gaiety, and on hot days providing a place of restful coolness as they undoubtedly did for hundreds of years in a native habitat. The dynamic movement of baroque sculpture which was to culminate in Bernini's exquisite fountains in Rome is all there. To get to the courtyard walk through the Coffman Memorial Union from the front.

Guthrie Theater

725 Vineland Place, Minneapolis. 377-2224.

The Guthrie Theater *as* theater is discussed in another section of this guidebook. Architecture is perhaps the most functional of the arts, and buildings are built for a purpose, and so it was that Ralph Rapson designed this one as a beautiful envelope to bring audience and players together. But buildings can of course be works of art themselves, though never in the abstract and without reference to the activities they serve. The best way to approach this theater building is slowly, and from across the expanse of lawn it faces, and at night during its season of repertory. Then its openness, articulated in the big glass areas set in concrete, with many balloonlike lamps and red doors alive behind the glass, announces that it is indeed a theater, that it is richly active, that the audience is welcome. Inside, the theater proper has seats upholstered in many colors, further proposing aliveness, and the two tiers of seats (main floor and balcony) are broken at one end by a steep bank of seats extending from stage level to the top, which avoids the composure of an unbroken amphitheater. Above, near the ceiling, are square "clouds" which seem modernistically to float. The remarkable thing inside and out is the degree to which stationary objects suggest the movement of drama.

IDS Tower and Center

Nicollet Mall and Eighth Street, Minneapolis. 372-3131.

The IDS Tower, looming fifty-seven stories high at the heart of the IDS Center, is the tallest building between Chicago and San Francisco. Designed by Philip Johnson, it is a shimmering octagonal giant swathed in a bluish glass, with a fascinating cut-back design on four sides providing thirty-two additional corner offices on each floor. From the observation floor, the viewer can gain a vista of up to thirty-five miles. When completed, a network of skyways will connect the various elements of the IDS complex with buildings on bordering streets. The Center will contain a hotel, a theater, and a Crystal Court, Middle America's twentieth-century version of London's Crystal Palace of 1851. The Court is an airy cascade of glass, steel, and plastic pyramids housing a restaurant, shops, and an exhibit area. Tours of the IDS Tower are scheduled to begin in late autumn of 1972.

Indian God of Peace

St. Paul City Hall and Ramsey County Courthouse, 15 West Kellogg Boulevard, St. Paul. 223-4012.

The most significant local mingling of our Scandinavian and American artistic heritages looms thirty-six feet high in the St. Paul City Hall and Ramsey County Courthouse. Set against a backdrop of black onyx and carved of white Mexican onyx, Carl Milles' peace monument recalls pre-Columbian sculpture and yet is a completely contemporary work of art. It was completed in 1936, and while the legend on which it is based seems naively hopeful today it is worth citing to give an idea of the theme: "As a group of Indians crouch about their council fire smoking the pipe of peace, the smoke arising heavenward takes the form of an Indian God of Peace, one hand holding a peace pipe, the other extended in a gesture of friendliness, symbolic of the thought that out of the conference and understanding comes the hope of peace in the world." The statue was cut in 98 blocks and joined in 38 sections, but the effect of one giant block is successfully achieved. This is enhanced by its not being carved fully in the round: legs are merely suggested and the rigidity of primitive sculpture is there, intensifying the total effect of peace, calm, and hope. The five figures of the Indians which form the base are engaged to the pedestal, in an attitude suggesting their fervent desire for peace. The statue oscillates on a turntable in a part circle, each rotation taking two and one half hours, "as though summoning the world from every point of the compass to a great peace council." (Meyric R. Rogers.) If you are fortunate enough to arrive when the peace monument is at an angle, allowing you to examine the back, be certain to do so, as it forms a totem pole with small figures in relief, very suggestive of American Indian art. Walk up to the second and third floors in order to view the details and for a closer inspection of the Indian's majestic head. This is highly recommended in a tour of St. Paul.

Minneapolis City Hall– Hennepin County Courthouse

Fourth to Fifth Street and Third to Fourth Avenue South, Minneapolis.

With its steeply pitched roofs, conical gables, massive clock tower, and rock-faced granite this building might well be seen as the quiet twin to St. Paul's Federal Courts Building. It was designed by Long and Kees of Minneapolis and built between 1889 and 1905. Although he finds it a less subtle building than its source, H. H. Richardson's Allegheny County Buildings at Pittsburgh, Donald Torbert asserts that it is "a building of power and dignity which has for a long time not been properly appreciated." (*Significant Architecture in the History of Minneapolis*.)

Minnesota State Capitol

Cedar and Aurora Streets, St. Paul. 296-2881 (tours).

The work of such architects as Louis Sullivan, Marcel Breuer, Ralph Rapson, and Minoru Yamasaki in Minnesota will doubtless prove over time to be of more enduring interest than that of Cass Gilbert, who designed the state capitol in 1894–95, but Gilbert and his building are of at least some historical importance. Forty-one firms entered the competition for the commission. Gilbert's winning entry was — as Donald Torbert writes in *A History of the Arts in Minnesota*, — "a monument in the 'Renaissance' tradition. . . . The use of a great Michelangelesque drum and dome above a central pavilion, with flanking wings and terminal pavilions capped by lower and flatter domes over the legislative chambers, had an immediate precedent in McKim, Mead and White's capitol for the state of Rhode Island at Providence. There was nothing in the design which could be dubbed 'midwestern.' The Minnesota capitol was under construction from 1896 to 1905; the materials and the workmanship were excellent and the decorations were lavish.'' Gilbert designed many other buildings, including the United States Supreme Court in Washington, and it is inconceivable that American architectural history could be written without mentioning him. His state capitol in St. Paul must be allowed its impressiveness. But it *is* deriva- tive. Nevertheless, it should be visited — as well for its place as a seat of government as for historical interest. The American sculptor Daniel French, who did the immense statue for the Lincoln Memorial in Washington, created six heroic figures on the exterior of the Minnesota State Capitol. Tours are available, or one may visit the building oneself.

Northwestern National Life Insurance Building

20 Washington Avenue South, Minneapolis. 372-5432.

The Northwestern National Life Insurance Company's choice of Minoru Yamasaki as architect for its new domicile in the early 1960's has done much to enliven the safety-first image which clings to the insurance business. And for- tunately, the civic-minded Northwestern management offers weekday tours to the public. Yamasaki has stated that ''the challenge was to find a concept appropriate to the site — the focal point of the Gateway Center redevelopment — which would serve as a terminus for Nicollet Avenue.'' And this he has dramatically achieved, with a six-story portico as the entry to a latter-day Greek temple with attenuated arches, into which are inserted Vermont verde antique marble, the architect having chosen a minimum of glass because of the climate. The portico is enhanced by flowering trees, a pool and sculpture by Nagare of Tokyo done in Swedish black granite.

One trouble with being an employee of Northwestern is that one cannot have the lovely exterior in sight, but compensation exists, for "restraint," "subtlety," "civilization" are the key words for the interior. A low-keyed entryway with white marble floors, green rug, one green plant, and two or three pots of *fresh* flowers (the rule throughout the building) is capped by Bertoia's sculptured "Sunlight Straw" to reflect the agricultural area of the state. The arch of windows is echoed in various ways in the interior, most impressively in the baroque ovoid curve of the white marble hallways. All offices are on the outside of the building, so that the light and airy feeling of the exterior prevails. They are a bit too anonymous in their no-color sort-of beiges, but Yamasaki's desire to have the focus on people rather than things has been achieved. The tour includes the inevitable dead spots, reassuring sights of all those policies carefully filed, and the printing and medical offices, etc. Save your energy and concentration for the sixth floor, which houses the executive offices and employees' cafeteria and lounge.

Here the carefully selected fabrics and woods are allowed to speak for themselves; fussy details which too often have crept right back into modern décor have been eliminated. Our favorite is the Board Room with its ebony doors, rosewood table (which mirrors the hallway-window shape), and teak panelling, complemented by maroon tweed chairs, and black leather-reddened chairs. But not to be ignored are the cafeteria, a sunny room with peach, yellow, and orange fabric on the walls, and the employees' lounge, where the lush reds and purples of Birney Quick's painting of a peacock are reflected in the colors of the room. The building is of course a "must" for architectural students and architectural buffs, but is much recommended to anyone who wants to see one of our most beautiful buildings.

Alfred Pillsbury Residence

116 East Twenty-second Street, Minneapolis.

Charles S. Pillsbury Residence

100 East Twenty-second Street, Minneapolis.

Combine a trip to the Minneapolis Institute with a walking tour of nearby buildings. This could include a visit to the First Christian Church (see description in this section) and observation from outside of the former homes of Charles and Alfred Pillsbury. Number 116, the Alfred Pillsbury Residence, dates from 1903, and is built of rock-faced limestone in the so-called "English gothic" style which was often a mixture of Tudor, Elizabethan, and Jacobean elements, but which in this case happily sidestepped the riot of ornament one finds in many residences built at the turn of the century. On the adjoining lot the more elegant Charles Pillsbury residence, built in 1912, is made of dressed limestone, with more refinements in elegant gables, and stone-carved heraldic shields, but, as Donald Torbert has pointed out in *Significant Architecture in the History of Minneapolis*, "both houses use ornamental detail sparingly, clearly [showing] the geometric nature of the several parts, and use transoms, mullions, and string courses to tie the elements into a whole that is simple, solid and dignified." The buildings are currently used as offices by the Minneapolis Institute of Arts and are not open to the public.

Prince of Peace Lutheran Church for the Deaf

205 Otis Avenue, St. Paul. 644-9804.

Form should express function, argued the American architect Louis Sullivan, and this church for the deaf seems designed to follow that sensible precept admirably. The interior is relatively small, the sight lines for the congregation appear good, and there is ample light provided, even on a darkish day, by the extensive use of glass as one of the building materials. Symbolically and esthetically, the church is also quietly successful. A cluster of crosses — three in number, each with a different height, and in black and gold — stands in front of the church. Another, smaller cross, its only unfortunate aspect being that it is on an odd metal base, surmounts the building. The most arresting feature of the church is the effect of overlaid patterns. This is afforded, as one contemplates the façade, by a metal screen in which circles are mingled with crosses (each circle symbolizing heaven), and beyond which are seen as additional layers the glass on either side of the church interior, glass in which vertical supports contrast with the circles of the screen. It can further be said that, while the elements are certainly Christian, there is also, curiously, a handsome Saracenic or Moorish aspect to the screen with its delicate tracery. The church was designed by Ralph Rapson, who is also director of the School of Architecture at the University of Minnesota. He has created a beautifully subdued jewelbox.

The Promise to Youth

Outside Veterans' Service Building, Capitol Approach, St. Paul.

Alonzo Hauser, who now lives and has his studio in Prescott, Wisconsin, has been a major force in the arts for many years. Though he is an interesting painter, he is best known as a sculptor, one of his principal successes being his eloquent human faces and figures. His *Promise to Youth* is the bronze figure of a girl inside the petals of a large flower, which can unfold slowly as the figure rises and as water comes forth. (Inquire about the times of opening of the sculpture.) The figure is largely hidden by the petals when they are folded, but even then it is beautiful in its chrysalislike quiet. Controversy swirled around the sculpture for some time, because there were those who were shocked to think of a nude figure on the capitol grounds. What would they have felt if they had lived in ancient Greece?

St. John's Abbey and University Church

Collegeville, 85 miles north of Twin Cities.

This is quite simply the most beautiful building in Minnesota. It was designed by Marcel Breuer, who was born in Hungary in 1902 and during the 1920's was associated with the Bauhaus, the famous art school in Germany. Construction of the church at St. John's to his design was completed in 1961. It stands on a hill among, but not crowded in by, other St. John's buildings, and the setting is enhanced by the presence nearby of a lake. An immense, free-standing concrete bell banner presents an effective contrast to the façade of the church; both are strong, but the façade is honeycombed by stained-glass windows by Bruno Bak, suggesting the disappearance of structural elements in favor of light for a shining church. Inside, there is first a baptistry, which has the effect of an enclosed courtyard. A bronze figure of John the Baptist, by Doris Caesar, gestures toward the font. Next one enters the church proper, whose focal point is an altar, over which a baldachino is suspended. Far above there is light, perhaps suggestive of heaven, from windows in the ceiling. And as a backdrop for the altar there is a large red screen to the rear of the choir area. Surrounding all of this in the broad, deep church are brick floors, handsome dark benches, and huge concrete folds in the walls. Looking back from the altar area, one sees the large balcony cantilevered from four large piers, and the interior of the honeycombed façade window with its gradations of color leading from each side toward what seems (subtly) to be a rose window in the center. Perhaps the bells outside will ring as you are about to leave, making a lovely muted sound in the church, and adding the impression of music to the splendid combination of modern strength of form with an almost Berniniesque play of light and color.

No other entry in this guidebook takes one as far from the Twin Cities. But then, no other building is as remarkable. Write The Benedictines, Collegeville, Minnesota 56321, for information.

St. Mary's Greek Orthodox Church

3450 Irving Avenue South, Minneapolis. 825-9595.

One of the most unusual and successful transplantations of an architectural form indigenous to a very different culture and climate can be found on the shores of Lake Calhoun in a bit of Byzantium brought to Minneapolis. St. Mary's Greek Orthodox Church has a golden dome atop a structure of muted beige brick, some of whose walls are punctured by small rectangular windows reminiscent of an Eastern European monastery or church. The church edifice represents the universe, with the dome as the arch of heaven. Stressing the risen, triumphant Christ rather than the suffering Christ, the Eastern Church, both in iconography and in its buildings, has an air of Christ as King. Both the exterior and interior convey this. The architects, Thorshov and Cerny, were particularly fortunate to have spacious grounds with beautiful old trees for their setting. Walk around the church and its attendant buildings, in order to study the effect of the sun glinting off the gold cross and dome. Twilight is a particularly stirring time for this. The interior is built on the form of the Greek cross, with light coming from three sides so that one's eyes are carried to the altar with its striking painting of the Virgin Mary in the manner of Giotto or Cimabue. The interior is surprisingly light, considering the size of the windows. Blue, gold, and white predominate, for the stress here is upon the church as a palace of God. The circle motif of the dome is carried out in a pair of double-ringed candelabra, and in a particularly handsome gold altar screen, while the Byzantine style of painting predominates in the single row of stained glass windows on the ground level, and in several groupings of small paintings depicting scenes from the life of Christ.

St. Peter's Lutheran Church

5421 France Avenue South, Edina. 927-8408.

In a metropolitan area which abounds in interesting modern church architecture this building designed by Ralph Rapson in 1957–58 remains one of the outstanding examples of form and function coalescing into a dramatic symbol of Christianity. The building is organized on the octagon, the symbol of the eight souls who were saved from the Flood, as well as of the church as an eight-faceted gem. The turn away from the idea of the church as a fortress shielding its members from the world, to the view that it should actively participate in worldly affairs, is aptly symbolized in the airy lightness and openness of the building, with the heavens pouring in to reveal God. A church publication states that "the superstructure of the Church according to St. Peter is built up of lively stones of the individual believers, who are radiant with the light of God's indwelling Holy Spirit and 'show forth the praises of Him who has called them out of darkness into His marvelous light.' This is suggested by the eight triangular windows facing out in every direction of the compass, which not only allow 'the heavens to declare God's glory and the firmament to reveal His handiwork' to a worshipping congregation but also to remind them of Christ's great commission to go and teach all nations, to let the Gospel light shine before men.'' Rapson has placed colored strips in translucent windows so that the effect of the jewels is achieved but light abounds. The altar is sited in the very center of the church, with a circular seating for the congregation to emphasize the Protestant doctrine that believers need no priest to intercede between the individual and God, but stressing particularly the Lutheran church organization where the congregation is the unit of organization and the seat of authority. The drama of the altar is enhanced both by its centrality and by the simple but forceful juxtaposition of white and black: the white marble altar is set on a black octagon, which in turn is supported by a white marble pedestal.

The Source

Rice Park, near Public Library, St. Paul.

The female figure, created by the sculptor Alonzo Hauser, represents sources — of rivers, of government, perhaps of life itself. It is not a pioneer woman, as some have suggested. The sculpture is set in one of those pleasant small parks that every city should have in abundance, as oases of repose.

Walker Art Center

Vineland Place, Minneapolis. 377-7500.

This building, designed by Edward Larabee Barnes and selected as one of nine buildings to receive the 1972 Honor Awards of the American Institute of Architects, has been dubbed "an elegant warehouse" by New York art critic Hilton Kramer, and this is not too far off the mark. But Kramer also regards it as better than Frank Lloyd Wright's Guggenheim Museum in New York. One is confronted at the Walker with a mass of lavender brick, relieved occasionally with a large banner announcing a current show. Windows are nonexistent, as the building is designed to allow for a controlled environment in which to display modern art. Since the new Walker building was designed to adjoin the Guthrie Theater, Barnes may well have had in mind the striking contrast his monolithic structure makes with the openness of Ralph Rapson's façade for the Guthrie, as well as the functional needs of an art gallery. For a description of the interior, see the entry for the Walker Art Center in our Museums and Art Galleries section.

Annuals, Perennials, and Occasionals

There are events which enter the scene once a year or at other intervals. We have where possible listed a telephone number from which information on a particular event's timing may be sought. And announcements typically appear in the Minneapolis and St. Paul newspapers.

he Source" by Alonzo Hauser

Festival of Nations

International Institute, 1694 Como Avenue, St. Paul. 647-0191.

The Festival of Nations, offered at about three-year intervals, has a simulated International Village with representative buildings created for individual nations. There are displays of folk crafts, food of various places can be sampled, and perhaps most colorful of all are the folk dances: Hungarian czardas, Irish jigs, the Highland fling, Polish polkas, and Scandinavian steps. For details on time and place, telephone the Institute.

Minneapolis Aquatennial

Office: 15 South Fifth Street, Minneapolis. 332-7412.

Since 1940 the Minneapolis Aquatennial has provided a summer complement to its twin's winter carnival, and though it is by now a distinctly amphibious creature, the city lakes still play host to certain events such as the pontoon boat lake cruise, sailing regattas, milk carton boat races and of course, water ski tournament. The Admiral's Ball, square dance, parades, and Queen of the Lakes Coronation and Ball are among the splashier events. But for the last six years the Aquatennial has been presenting the pageant of the seven seas, and in one year went Asiatic with a salute to the Indian Ocean, giving demonstrations of crafts, foods, dances, and fashions from a variety of nations. The Aquatennial activities are so varied that one would do well to inquire in advance from the Aquatennial Association about times and locations of particular activities, as some of the more interesting events get less newspaper coverage than the juvenilia such as waiters and waitresses racing with trays of glasses.

Minnesota Renaissance Fair

Held annually during part of September near Jonathan.

The Minnesota Art League (telephone 920-3363) sponsors this delightful and evocative fair whose incarnation in 1971 was so successful, with 40,000 visitors on two weekends, that plans were made for its continuation with a tripled area. The setting was wooded and open slopes through which one wended one's way, out of sight of one's automobile, and past more than 100 booths at which artists displayed and sold their prints, pottery, and other work. There was surprisingly little kitsch. Most of the artists were clad in Renaissance costumes, and while we have been known to object to period costumes on a restaurant's staff, because the costumes there do not accompany an altogether authentic ambience, the tents and stalls on the rolling land near Jonathan were essentially of a piece with what one imagines similar land near, say, Salisbury, England, to have been. Musicians strolled about, food and drink were offered in tents, fencing and archery and other Renaissance sports were available for visitors' participation, a company of actors on a rough stage in a pleasant field gave us some scenes from *A Midsummer Night's Dream*, and caparisoned horses carried costumed riders about. On a warm September day this becomes quite idyllic as atmosphere, as experience. Later, it is memory, perhaps aided by the presence of an impressionistic print of a medieval townscape or a handmade earth-brown coffee mug one purchased at a modest price. The fair, then, is no gaudy carnival. It is a surprisingly successful evocation of a collective European past.

Minnesota State Fair

State Fair Grounds, St. Paul.

This yearly bash, which sprawls over countless acres between the University of Minnesota's St. Paul campus and Snelling Avenue, offers in late August and very early September an array of entertainment (carnival shows and rides, auto racing, equestrian spectacles, etc.), industrial exhibits, food (mostly of the quick-lunch variety), informational displays by government, educational, military, and other organizations, and much else. For the citybred, whose close-up knowledge of farming is apt to be pretty minimal, the pavilions where prize sheep, swine, cattle, horses, and other animals can be seen are consistently the most interesting part of the Fair. Families with young children may wish to look as well for the mobile home displays, if our experience with their attractions for our sons is any guide. And note, in keeping track of children, that the Fair has incredible magnetism for people from all over the state, with the inevitable result that crowds can be vast at popular hours in good weather. The State Fair has little to nourish artistic interests, but it is a quintessential expression of American life, and we recommend one visit for as long as your feet hold out. Return visits can be made or not at one's discretion.

Norway Day

Though little of the Twin Cities' architecture or restaurant offerings suggests the extent of the Scandinavian heritage, a deep pride in this heritage and a determination to recreate certain aspects of it have inspired yearly festivals such as Norway Day, Svenskarnas Dag, and Finnish-American Day. Indeed, Minneapolis houses the international headquarters for the Sons of Norway organization. Both Norwegian Independence Day on May 17 and Norway Day, on the second Sunday in July, are celebrated. Norway Day is usually marked in Minnehaha Park, with a children's flag parade, colorfully dressed Norwegian folk dancers, musical groups, and individual musicians livening up the more staid events such as the address by a well-known speaker. Even if you cannot dredge up one Scandinavian forebear be certain to drop in on one of these public celebrations for the pleasant, old-fashioned sight of several generations of Americans who have happily nurtured two cultures. For more information about Norway Day contact the Sons of Norway, 1455 West Lake Street, Minneapolis. 827-3611.

Rose Fête

At Mpls. Institute of Arts and Washburn Fair Oaks Park across Twenty-fourth Street from the Institute.

This is an annual extravaganza of the popular arts which spreads itself one day in June over the Institute's lawn and interior and the rolling grounds of the park opposite, and sometimes over blocked-off streets (which ought everywhere in the Twin Cities more often be in this way committed to people, not cars). The idea of offering the arts directly to the community, not only inside the museums and in outreach programs, but in fairs like this and the Renaissance Fair in the fall, is what may pry people loose from their television sets and radios, thank god. To be sure, the first aspect of the Fête to reach your senses as you approach it is the rock music (superamplified of course), but there soon swim into your ken the other elements: a balloon-like tent for kids, art and handcraft stalls (we noted especially Peter Leach's pottery), old films, a flea market, the Shakespeare in the Streets company doing *Much Ado about Nothing*,

Greek music and dancing, a fashion show, the Minnesota Dance Theater performing, and much else. And people strolling everywhere, as much a part of the scene in *their* clothes (ranging from relaxed bare-midriff fashions to conservative vested suits) as the arts. The whole thing is superbly alive.

St. Paul Winter Carnival

Office: 143 West Fourth Street, St. Paul. 222-4416.

The big, annual, ten-day, extravagandistic *Do* in St. Paul is, of course, the Winter Carnival, with a five-hundred-mile snowmobile race (which starts in Winnipeg) and a King Boreas Banquet, Coronation, and Ball, followed by the Crowning of his queen. There is also a treasure hunt in which a Boreas Medallion worth up to $3,000, sponsored by the St. Paul Dispatch-Pioneer Press is hunted out via daily newspaper clues. Other neo-Mike Toddish events are the world's original ice-fishing contest, the nation's oldest hot air balloon race, a ski bob race, and sled-dog and -mutt races, all climaxed by the Fire King Torchlight Parade when to quote the Winter Carnival Association's literature, "Vulcanus Rex and his Krewe set the stage for the storming of Boreas' Ice Palace at the Parade."

Svenskarnas Dag

Each year, on (deo volente) a fair day in June, residents of a Swedish persuasion gather in Minnehaha Park in Minneapolis, where, under big trees hung with flags bearing the Swedish gold cross against a blue field and with the American stars and stripes, there are folk dancing, speeches, and other observances of Svenskarnas Dag. The dances are performed on a platform by sprightly, Nordic-featured men and women in full folk costume, to the accompaniment of a small orchestra, including a fiddle and accordion, while spectators applaud from benches arranged in a hemicycle around the platform. It is a sight suggestive not only of what one understands of Sweden in past centuries, but also of America's small-town heritage, when life centered on the town park or green. Whether one will want to devote long hours to Svenskarnas Dag will depend on the extent of one's interest and one's stamina, but a visit should be considered. Souvenirs and refreshments are available for the so-minded.

Uptown Art Fair

Hennepin Avenue and Lake Street business district, Minneapolis.

One of the largest and longest-lived city art fairs, this has in recent years swelled to proportions where more than three hundred exhibitors from a dozen states have shown and sold their wood carvings, jewelry, ceramics, stained and blown glass, pottery, oils, and water colors for several days. There is a certain amount of kitsch on sale, but also interesting pieces of art and handcrafts by such exhibitors as Donald Holmquist of St. Paul (small stone sculptures) and the Gilberts of Elk Mound, Wisconsin (gold and silver smithing). What make it difficult to appreciate even the good things at the height of the fair are the crowds which choke the narrow sidewalks in the area, except in a few quiet sidestreets. Still, there is everything to be said for taking the "cult" out of "culture," for getting art onto the sidewalks. Now, if only the streets themselves could be turned over to the art fair. . . .

Artists exhibiting must pay a $20 fee, and they are chosen

on a first-come-first-served basis because of space limitations. Sponsors of the fair are forty-seven business people in the Hennepin-Lake area.

Green Spaces

St. Paul Parks and Recreation Department

545 City Hall, St. Paul. 224-4612.

Minneapolis Parks and Recreation Department

250 South Fourth Street, Minneapolis. 348-2121.

Both cities have extensive park systems, thanks to the farsightedness and determination of such planners as Horace Cleveland and Charles Loring in the nineteenth century, and one of the most important results of early planning was a joint arrangement whereby riverside lands were kept for parks and driveways. The St. Paul Park system has 2,190 acres which are divided up into parks, parkways, playfields, and playgrounds. Minneapolis has 5,500 acres of park and water, the land consisting of triangles, parks, playgrounds, and land around the lakes. In both systems, tennis courts, swimming pools, golf courses, picnic tables, shelters, and ice skating areas are available, and both sponsor a variety of activities from yo-yo tournaments to summer concerts. The weekly activities in Minneapolis parks are listed in the Home and Recreation section of the *Minneapolis Sunday Tribune*. Check with the park departments for information about the parks most conveniently located for you. We mention here a few which we have found particularly interesting.

For a pleasant picnic and riverview hike, seek out the

strip of Minneapolis parkland which can be approached from the parking area on the West River Drive at East Thirty-sixth Street. Take the path down into a dell and up to the bluffs, where you will find picnic tables set in a clearing and a magnificent view of the river. You can hike from here along the river bluffs, although children should be closely watched. For that sort of urban-rusticity where nature really is improved by art, take the walk around Lake of the Isles. The largest of Minneapolis city parks, Theodore Wirth, is a vast wooded, hilly area providing city dwellers an opportunity to cast off cares and to swim and play golf. The charming Shingle Creek flows into the Mississippi near Forty-second Avenue North in Shingle Creek Park. Nearby there are paths, and a boat-launching ramp is located just south of the bridge. For the masochist-naturalist seeking a rugged walk, try the Father Hennepin Park, which has been hacked out of six acres along the river's edge near Main Street Southeast, largely by the volunteer help of teenagers. The park contains the rock from which Hennepin discovered St. Anthony Falls in 1680. Steep wooden steps lead down to the river, where mere hints of paths take you to a tangled island from which you can get a different vista of the Stone Arch Railroad Bridge (see Historic Sites). A few more twists and turns and battlings of brambles and you come upon a Piranesi veduta — broken walls surrounded by a lush over-growth, the Pillsbury ''A'' Mill looming in Italianate splendor, and perhaps two idyllic fishermen sitting on an abandoned wall. All this in the middle of the city, which is still evident aurally but is far away visually.

In St. Paul, Como Park is the Queen of the Twin Cities' parklands, for its multifaceted features and for its beauty. The largest of St. Paul parks, Phalen, has a sizable lake and golf course. But for a less obvious, more ruggedly beautiful park area, try Hidden Falls at Magoffin Avenue and Mississippi River Boulevard. Once again one rapidly leaves the city behind and finds a tangled area, safer for children than Father Hennepin Park. Parking lot and picnic tables are near the river, but best of all there is an opportunity for a close-up view of tug-pushed barges. Pleasant rambles along the river are quite safe and a good hiker's walk away are the falls themselves, near the Ford Bridge. Cherokee Heights Park, running along Cherokee Boulevard, provides a vast if somewhat depressing view of St. Paul. Battle Creek Park on Point Douglas Road has a canyonlike setting.

Walk over to Rice Park on a steamy summer day to watch your fellow mortals — some of whom may be cooling off in the fountain surrounding Alonzo Hauser's sculpture the Source — or to contemplate the French-Chateauish Federal Courts Building (for both see our section on Points of Artistic and Architectural Interest), or generally to consider what a civilized spot this is. In 1849 this was designated a public square by John R. Irvine and Henry Rice. Although its moment of glory came in 1883 when it served as the site of the reception given to mark the completion of the Northern Pacific Railroad, a reception attended by President Arthur and Generals Grant and Sherman, of equal importance is the opportunity it offers St. Paulites in the twilight of our more hectic century to relax in a pretty square in the midst of urban turmoil.

Special features of certain of these and other Minneapolis and St. Paul Parks are among the entries below.

Eloise Butler Wild Flower Garden

Glenwood Avenue and Abbott Avenue North, Theodore Wirth Park, Minneapolis. 374-4305.

Wild-flower fanciers and any others who want a temporary sanctuary from the insistences of city living will find this charming garden, which is only a short drive from the center of Minneapolis, nearly ideal. Species of flowers abound in their season, growing in conditions very like those of an untouched and wooded rural valley, and there are discreet labels to identify them for you as you wend your way along the paths. A limited amount of parking is available not far from the garden's entrance. Observe, too, the rolling green acres of Theodore Wirth Park nearby, waiting for picnickers or walkers.

Canoe and Bike Rentals, Lake Calhoun Boathouse

West Lake Street and Lake Calhoun Boulevard, Minneapolis. 823-8386.

A nice balance to a day in a city office can be a canoe trip through the chain of lakes from Lake Calhoun to Lake of the Isles and Cedar Lake. While you can't entirely shuck off noise pollution, a few minutes out into the middle of Lake of the Isles in particular will at least calm your ulcers and demonstrate just how beautiful a megatown can be. Prices are reasonable, as this is sponsored by the Minneapolis Park Board: for canoes, a $5.00 deposit, and 50¢ per 15 minutes, three passengers at a maximum in one canoe. If you are feeling a bit more energetic, try renting a bike for a ride around any one of the three lakes. Bikes too require the $5.00 deposit, and they cost 40¢ per 15 minutes for singles, 75¢ per 20 minutes for tandems.

Canoeing at William O'Brien State Park

North of Marine on St. Croix. Telephone Muller Boat Works in Stillwater. 439-5658 for information.

Several hours afloat on the St. Croix River are not only de rigeur at regular intervals for outdoor types; they are tonic to urban sorts who have been too long in the city and are coming up for air. The do-it-yourself plan at O'Brien, whereby one simply rents a canoe and paddles off whither one wills, is much to our relaxed and simple tastes. If your own tastes run in similar quiet channels, we recommend calling for information and then driving over. The O'Brien Park itself is pleasant, and after buying a state park sticker for your car (if you do not already possess one) you can proceed to the hut near the water from which, under an arrangement with the Park, an organization related to Muller Boat Works will rent canoes on the following basis: There is a $10.00 deposit. The first two hours of canoeing will cost you $3.00 plus tax; and prices thereafter move in steps to $9.00 plus tax for 8 hours. The facilities open by midmorning, with all canoes to be returned by 8 p.m., and they are in operation approximately from Memorial Day to Labor Day.

The river is usually flowing with a noticeable but not difficult current in this area — but watch for exceptional conditions — the banks are verdant in the summer and little populated, and pleasant islands (at least one with a sandy beach) abound. The canoes themselves are sturdily constructed of aluminum, and there is room in them for two paddlers plus, say, one passenger and picnic provisions. Caveat emptor: Unless you enjoy competing with motor-driven river traffic, you would be well advised to avoid canoeing on weekends or in the late afernoon.

Como Lake Canoe and Bike Rentals

Como Park Pavilion, St. Paul. Tel. 488-1477.

It's not quite the Bois du Boulogne, but it is one of the many parks which make city life so pleasant and if you rent a canoe at the Como Lake Pavilion you will see the swans which grace the lake in this lovely park. The price is $2.25 per hour, and there is a $1.00 deposit. The bikes, and there is much reason to see the park this way — rent for $2.25 an hour for tandems, a mere $1.00 per hour for singles. Courtesy, Ramsey County Park Board. Be certain to note the pleasant fountain nearby, particularly in the evening; a not terribly distinguished Indian maiden is surrounded by a ring of bright water.

Como Park Conservatory

Como Park, St. Paul. 489-1740.

One need not be a card-carrying gardener to enter here and revel in domesticated nature. Eyes and nose will do. The first encounter, in the entranceway, is with the small cactus gardens, where there is a complexly painted Sicilian burro cart as well. Next: The palm house, domed in steel and glass. Try to forget the Hawaiian muzak-type noise, and consider the palm trees, such as the Chinese fan palm thrusting up to the summit of the dome, and a splendid thick-trunked variety (un-nametagged) whose fronds burst like a chief's feathers from the top. The north house is the most successful wing of the conservatory, for here the effect is basically green, with a few flowers as accents, and the arrangement is studiedly informal. Among the species of trees and plants are a gnarled fig tree, a magnolia, and a grapefruit tree. The general impression is that of the so-called English garden — nature, as Alexander Pope said, improv'd by art. By contrast, the sunken garden room on the other side of the palm house is all geometricity, as in a seventeenth-century French garden by André Le Nôtre, with chrysanthemums or other flowers rank on rank around a key-shaped pool stocked with goldfish. The fern room, where ferns, mosses, ivies, and other green varieties grow over a rockery, is demure and pleasant. There are special floral displays in each season, utilizing the sunken garden and sometimes specially opened rooms at the back of the conservatory (thus, lilies and tulips and other flowers in the spring, poinsettias and cyclamens in the winter, for example). The staff can be consulted as to particulars of time and contents.

Landscape Arboretum of the University of Minnesota

Four miles west of Chanhassen on Highway 5.

The Arboretum is a laboratory in the sun (and sometimes rain). Its hundreds of acres near Excelsior are a research ground for ornamental trees, vines, shrubs and herbaceous plants, many of them not normally found in this area. Horticulturalists and their students test and breed plant varieties and develop them. Happily for the visitor, they are labeled and arranged in a setting of ponds and woods. The work of the staff is partly evident in the appearance of the Arboretum itself, but it also manifests itself in the information provided nurseries, scientists, schools, garden clubs, et al. Its history in this good work goes back to the 1950's, when the inspiration of the Minnesota State Horticultural Society led to the Arboretum's founding and establishment in the University's Department of Horticultural Science.

Whether of a botanical persuasion or not, you will want to consider visiting the Arboretum and walking over some of its rolling acres, with their woodlands, meadows, and cultivated areas. There is a picnic ground as well. One should not, of course, expect in the Arboretum as a whole the untouched aspect of a remote part of a state park. Man has been here and left his mark. But neither is there the geometric, parade-order look of one of the well-manicured gardens at Versailles.

In sum, the Arboretum is useful scientifically, reasonably pleasant in appearance for the city-jaded, and certainly instructive for the plant-nik and gardener. Fee: $1.00 per car for nonmembers. Tours available by reservation. Inquire about hikes.

Minnehaha Falls

Minnehaha Park, Minneapolis.

Although he never actually set eyes on the meeting place of Hiawatha and his beloved Minnehaha, Longfellow must at least have gazed on an evocative painting of the falls, for they have all the romance needed for the meeting place of a culture hero and loved one. The falls are at their most dramatic and beautiful in winter when their beauty outshines that of any man-made ice-sculpture. But the summer months are the time to take a more leisurely amble along the creek to the waterfall. Skip the Park's not very interesting statue of the legendary characters and climb down a steep flight of steps just below the falls in order to see the falls from below. (Be warned: there are many more steps to go up than down!) A short walk along the creek takes you through a glen which belies its location in the heart of the city; in June it is studded with wild roses, forget-me-nots, and other wild flowers, and a nearly tropical growth of trees form a welcome refuge from the city streets. During the spring melt and the rains the laughing waters are apt to approximate Henry VIII's bellow rather than the delicate tinkle which the Bard of Brattle Street had in mind. After you have seen the falls from above and below, walk downstream along the creek toward the Mississippi River; the creek becomes shallow and wide, a boon to kids long in city pent. Here they can wade, splash, and build dams to their heart's delight. Children should be accompanied by an adult when walking to the falls as there are precipitous areas along the path. Minnehaha Park is one of the many fine parks in the Twin Cities, but because of its size it is apt to be crowded on weekends when large organizations often make use of it. Try a pleasant weekday stroll.

Queen of the Lakes, Sternwheeler

Lake Calhoun, West Lake Street and Lake Calhoun Boulevard. 823-8386.

On this diminutive sternwheeler you can take the youngsters for a trip on three lakes starting at the boathouse on Lake Calhoun and proceeding around Calhoun, through the channel to the queen of the city lakes, Lake of the Isles, and on through the bayou-like lagoon to Cedar Lake. The Queen has daily cruises in the summer months only. Prices are 50¢ per person for one- or two-lake cruises, $1.00 for the three-lake cruise. Information on hours or on charters can be obtained from telephoning.

Rose Garden, Lyndale Park

Near northeast corner of Lake Harriet, Minneapolis.

Here is a pleasant place in which to idle away an hour. Two fountains plash, tulips boldly fringe the fountain area, and beyond, when in the fullness of their season, are the many rows of roses among which to wander. Needless to say, the time of year has much to do with the success of a visit to the rose garden; but so also the day and hour, for the sense of order and composure here will be most apparent when few people are about. Parking is available nearby.

A Miscellany

In guidebooks, as in life, there are loose ends. But many of them are interesting, and there is here and there below a place or group that is truly one of a kind. This section, then, deserves close attention; there may be something here for everyone.

Como Zoo

Como Park, St. Paul. 488-3221 or 489-9815.

Unless and until the Twin Cities have an extensive new zoo with, perhaps, simulated natural habitats for the animals, this zoo in Como Park is it. In fact, it does have a number and variety of species that surprise when one thinks of the modest space available. A visit in warm weather is recommended, so that you can see the greatest number of animals outside. Among those owned by the zoo are owls, llamas, an elephant, peafowl, geese, and ducks, and there are seals in a pool encircling a monkey island. Children may wish to importune their parents to buy 15¢ packets of fish from a vendor hard by the seal pool, so that morsels can be tossed to the agile, barking animals below. At times elsewhere on the grounds, Sparky, a trained seal, displays his talents in shows. There is also a small primate house with gorillas, and a barnyard area sometimes inhabited by rustic species. Finally, there is the zoo building, housing various acrobatic monkeys, red-nosed Mandrill baboons, a jaguar lying on its back and staring fixedly at the ceiling, a lizard known as a Malayan water monitor which rhythmically flicks out its tongue, lions, tigers, etc. And a turtle or two moving glacially about the building's interior, so that kids can easily ride astride them. Some of the animals (all caged, of course) move through doors between the inside and outside; this, thank god, increases their pacing space, which is for some of them rather constricted.

There is no admission and a family visit is suggested. Younger members through, say, early teenage will no doubt head first before any thought is given to the zoo, to the adjacent amusement area when it is open; this is at the west end of the conservatory-zoo-amusements complex. Here there are — at one or two 10¢ per-child tickets per ride — Ferris wheels, a Mad Mouse, a merry-go-round, roller coasters, helicopters, gentle boats and cars etc. Nearby (and free), are an old steam engine to gaze at and an old fire engine to climb on.

Film Societies and Series

Some of the Twin Cities' film series, such as those sponsored by the Bell Museum of Natural History and the Science Museum of Minnesota, stress nature films, while those given at the Minneapolis Public Library and the American Swedish Institute run to travel films, but by far the greatest number of the groups listed here concentrate on worthwhile old American and foreign films, and in a few cases you will be able to see great works by foreign producers which the commercial chains don't seem to run at any time. Watch for listings such as those in the Sunday Arts Section of the *Minneapolis Tribune*, or make a phone call to put yourself on a mailing list in the case of organizations which have telephone numbers.

Acme Film Society, 7½ East Twenty-sixth Street, Minneapolis. 825-9953.

American Swedish Institute, 2600 Park Avenue, Minneapolis. 335-7621.

Bell Museum of Natural History, Seventeenth and University Avenues, Minneapolis. 373-2423.

Bijou Film Society, 2829 Hennepin Avenue, Minneapolis.

Flem Film Society, 1661 Grand Avenue, St. Paul.

Grande Illusion Cinema, 416 Cedar Avenue, (Cedar Village Theater), Minneapolis. 335-0339.

Hamline University. Hewitt Avenue and Snelling Avenue North, St. Paul. 641-6221.

Macalester College, Olin Auditorium. Grand Avenue and Snelling Avenue South, St. Paul. 647-6221.

Minneapolis Institute of Arts, 201 East 24th Street, Minneapolis. 339-7661.

Minneapolis Public Library, 300 Nicollet Mall, Minneapolis. 372-6500. Some films are shown at Heritage Hall, but inquire about both children's and adult films at branch libraries.

Piper Film Club, 3404 Lyndale Avenue South, Minneapolis. 823-8676.

Saint Catherine College, Jeanne d'Arc Auditorium, St. Paul.

Science Musuem of Minnesota, 30 East Tenth Street, St. Paul. 222-6303.

Schubert Club Film Series, 30 East Tenth Street, St. Paul. 222-6122 or 227-8241.

University Film Society

Walker Art Center, Vineland Place, Minneapolis. 377-7500.

Xanadu Film Festival, Lutheran Student Center, Eleventh and University Avenues Southeast, Minneapolis. 331-7616.

Grain Exchange

Fourth Avenue and Fourth Street, Minneapolis. 336-6361.

The Minneapolis Grain Exchange is the largest cash grain market in the world, the volume of trading on the cash market averaging 1,000,000 bushels daily. The best time to arrive is shortly before 9:30 A.M., for the grain brokers in the pit shout their orders in seeming disorder when the opening bell rings. But as written explanations in the visitors' gallery point out, it is all done according to rule, for buyers and sellers are required to indicate their bids by open outcry. Each trader is his own auctioneer; the hand palm out indicates an offer to sell, while a palm in is a bid to buy. Even fractions of a cent can be signaled by fingers — for example, one finger equals one-eighth of a cent. Above the pit, markers post quotations on the blackboard, and elsewhere ticker-tapes provide a counterpoint to the swirl of activity. Visitors may observe this scene from the visitors' balcony; more extensive tours of the Exchange can be arranged for groups. Observe the exterior of the South Building with its handsome terra cotta ornamentation, for it is based on Louis Sullivan's Wainwright Building in St. Louis.

Guild of Performing Arts

504 Cedar Avenue, Minneapolis. 333-8269.

The Guild of Performing Arts, an artistic omnium-gatherum, is in its own way a microcosm of the artistic ferment in the macrocosm of the Twin Cities. It is the base of the Nancy Hauser Dance Company and School of Dance, and of the Guild's Music School, and under its auspices there is presented a music series entitled Opus Musicale, an umbrella term for a variety of concerts by professional and student musicians. In recent seasons the Guild has sponsored such guitarists as Michael Hauser, with his fine renderings of flamenco and classical music, and Dan Glass and Jeffrey Van performing classical guitar pieces. Poetry readings and occasional jazz concerts add to the rich mix of Guild offerings for either the participant or the spectator, while performing artists themselves may want to inquire about theater workshops and the opportunities to learn the Indian dance known as barata natyam, which is taught at the Guild. A telephone call will put you on the Guild's mailing list.

International Institute

1624 Como Avenue, St. Paul. 647-0191.

Best known for its Festival of Nations, the Institute is a nonpolitical, interfaith, interracial social agency offering assistance to immigrants on naturalization and immigration procedures as well as courses in conversational English. The Institute has the twofold aim of aiding new Americans to move into daily life and at the same time preserving distinctive cultural and national characteristics. In a sense, its goal is a mosaic, rather than a melting pot which has too often meant a blurring of lines into a bland neutrality (or a tasteless, unidentifiable stew). Foreign-language classes at the Institute frequently include opportunities to study Finnish, Spanish, French, German, Swedish, Norwegian, Italian, and Russian, and there are folk dances, craft classes in international caning, wycinanki (Polish paper cutting), rosemaling, and macramé. For all of these one pays a modest sum after joining the Institute for the nominal fee of $4.00 per family. On Wednesdays the Institute serves a luncheon concentrating on the food of one nation or an international mixture. These are open to the public. (For details, see our restaurant section.)

The Institute recently moved to its present site, which,

though disappointingly twentieth-century neutral in style, has been brightened by wall displays of craft work from various countries. Its postage-stamp-size gift shop offers for sale Ecuadorian scarves (at extremely reasonable prices), Ecuadorian wooden statues, Portuguese copper ware, Mexican tinware, macramé hangings, flags from various nations, and international cookbooks. For a description of The Festival of Nations, see our section on Annuals, Perennials, and Occasionals.

Jonathan Padelford, Sternwheeler

Departing from Harriet Island, St. Paul. 439-3555.

A round trip on the delightfully nostalgic sternwheeler Jonathan Padelford from Harriet Island to Fort Snelling takes approximately one and one-half hours and proves to be an exhilarating experience, especially for the younger members of the family. The boat itself is a treat — a 1970 recreation of its nineteenth-century forebears, it is a delightful two decker wedding cake trimmed in lacey gold, playing hurdy-gurdy tunes. While the stretch of river it traverses is anything but glamorous, there is something to be said for seeing the *working* river, barges tied up or being pushed by a tug, sand gravel companies, an NSP plant, oil docks, grain elevators en route, as well as mushroom caves. Downtown St. Paul is not exactly Gotham in profile, but the distant view from the boat is a new one. The huge red paddle aft attracts a continuing stream of youngsters, but eventually everyone can peer over for a spell as constant motion is the order of the day. When they tire of running about the top deck they can descend to the saloon snack bar — soft drinks, sandwiches, etc., are on sale. The bar is delightfully outfitted in Restrained Schmaltz style, evoking the Padelford's more elegant progenitors. The narration rates A plus for its avoidance of the twin horrors of most excursions — limp jokes and lists of benumbing statistics. Some solid information is offered about early inhabitants and the history of river life, as well as about Fort Snelling. Be warned about two things: The boat does not stop at the fort; it approaches it and the view is not too satisfactory, and be certain to wear warm clothing. This trip is recommended as a family outing. The River Excursions Company has another boat to be chartered out of Stillwater.

Prices on the Jonathan Padelford: $2.50 for adults, $1.50 for children. Excursions at a discount rate to groups of twenty-five or more with advance paid reservation. Also available for charter. Telephone for information about months, days and times of operation.

Lake Harriet Trolley

Forty-second Street and West Lake Harriet Boulevard, Minneapolis. 348-2243.

Young people and devotees of the arts of transportation will enjoy the short ride on Car No. 1300, vintage 1908, of a brave yellow hue, departing near the southwestern corner of Lake Harriet. Today the power is supplied by a flatcar attached to one end of the trolley, and the overhead wires are gone, but otherwise all is essentially as it must have been when this Como-Harriet line was part of a 523-mile network of the Twin City Rapid Transit Electric Railway, which ran in Minneapolis, St. Paul, and the suburbs until 1954. The resurrection is the work of the Minnesota Transportation Museum and the Minneapolis Parks and Recreation Board, which operate the trolley during the summer months. Fares are modest — 20¢ for adults and 10¢ for children under twelve, who must be accompanied by adults. Open approximately May 30 to September 1. Telephone for information on days and hours.

Minneapolis Star and Tribune Tour.

425 Portland Avenue, Minneapolis. 372-4141.

By calling in advance, one can arrange to take a tour of a number of the facilities of the newspaper's building on Portland Avenue. (It is not necessary, by the way, to form a group in order to do this. Families were welcomed when we were there.) First, there is a brief introduction by a guide, and this is followed by visits to such places as the composing room, where type is set, the facilities for making curved plates for the rotary presses, the printing presses themselves, a distribution area, etc. The guide explains the processes involved along the way, and in this way visitors can get a rough idea of many though not all of the steps in newspapering. And the number of people seen at work suggests well the immense concentration of staff time necessary to move the paper to press rapidly. Children will find the trip informative and not exhausting; it lasts about an hour.

Sand Burr Gulch

In back of Stagecoach Theater, Highway 101 between Savage and Shakopee.

Sand Burr Gulch is truly evocative of the raw, dusty main street of a western town, circa 1865. In the telegraph office the message of Lincoln's murder is arriving, while down the street in the barbershop a hobo song is followed by a sudden opening of a door to reveal a cowboy, fully dressed, sitting in a wooden bathtub. In the jailhouse, of course, prisoners play guitars and whittle in pastoral inno-cence, and across the street Doc Adams is versatile enough to take on "man and beast." Osgood's Mercantile Shop has "coffins, caskets, shrouds, English bulldogs, self-cocking revolvers, and Hercules Giant Powder'' as well as all of the other necessities of life on the frontier. Admission is 25¢ for children, 50¢ adults. Nearby a chuck wagon sells franks, soft drinks, etc. The game room in a building separate from Sand Burr Gulch can be skipped.

University of Minnesota Programs

Minneapolis and St. Paul campuses.

The University is a cultural resource of consequence. In addition to having its own performing groups, some of which we discussed in our Music and Theater sections, and besides having a Gallery, which is included in our Museums and Art Galleries, the University presents many public lectures, performances of music and dance, and other events, in large part through its Concerts and Lectures Department, whose telephone number is 373-2345. Among the events are two series offered under the banner of the University Artists Course: the Masterpiece Series, with New York's Pro Musica group, the Royal Winnipeg Ballet, guitarist Andres Segovia, pianist Andre Watts, and others; and the World Dance Series, including Les Ballets Africains, the Alvin Ailey American Dance Theater, the Beryozka Dance Company of Moscow, Bejart's Ballet of the Twentieth Century, and (again) the Royal Winnipeg. Season tickets for the Artists Course series allow savings as against individual-performance ticket prices. Information may be obtained from the University, and local newspapers can be watched for news of events. There are programs of some kinds at the University in the summer as well as during the regular academic year.

Afro-American Cultural Arts Center

24 East Thirty-first Street, Minneapolis. 827-5891.

The Afro-American Cultural Arts Center, a project of the Sabathani Community Center, is a creative expression of black awareness, with a particular stress upon cultural enrichment. This takes the form of musical instruction, theater classes, and dance instruction, and the Center houses an art gallery, museum, and library. The Center has sponsored Ronald Holbrook's Feast of the Circle Dancers, a company which specializes in African and Afro-American dance, a field opened up only within recent years by such notables as Pearl Primus and Percival Brode. The Feast of the Circle Dancers toured Africa in the summer of 1972 in addition to giving local performances. Like the Guild of Performing Arts, the Afro-American Center is another manifestation of the cultural growth taking place in the Twin Cities. While the Center's thrust is toward artistic development for minority groups, anyone is welcome to participate in its activities. A telephone call will place you on the Center's mailing list.

Fountain by Pietro Tacca, University of Minnesota

Index